fast and fresh with
saladXPRESS™

Over 150 Delicious Recipes for Salads,
Main Dishes, Desserts & More

fast and fresh with

saladXPRESS™

Over 150 Delicious Recipes for Salads,
Main Dishes, Desserts & More

amy merydith

Pascoe Publishing, Inc.
Rocklin, California

WST2018

Published in the United States of America by

Pascoe Publishing, Inc.

Rocklin, California

http://www.pascoepublishing.com

ISBN: 1-929862-34-2

04   05   10   9   8   7   6   5   4

Printed in Hong Kong

Table of Contents

Introduction

Two words describe the best salads—fast and fresh! Picture a chilled, crisp bed of salad greens garnished with an appetizing array of vegetables and splashed with a piquant dressing. A picture such as this makes your mouth water instantly, particularly on a warm summer day!

Inside the pages of this book you will find saladXPRESS™ recipes for a wonderful variety of salads including fruit, cole slaw, pasta, potato, field greens, marinated vegetable and many more. Each salad makes a healthful and delicious addition to your meal and many can be served as a full entrée, offering robust flavors and hearty portions. If you prefer classic recipes, try *Beef Ribeye Salad with Lemon Poppy Seed Dressing, Shredded Chicken Taco Salad* and *Crisp Green Salad with Herb Vinaigrette*. To enjoy a creative, new recipe you might choose *Gorgonzola Cheese & Walnut Potato Salad, Hawaiian Pineapple Cole Slaw* or *Chile Pepper Indian Cucumber Salad*. Each of the salads in this book will delight your family and friends.

The true beauty of a fast and fresh salad is your saladXPRESS™—it will grate, wash, dry and serve your salad with ease. But, the wonder of this appliance doesn't stop there. Try grilled sliced vegetables, potato pancakes, stir-fried vegetables and beef, hot soups, fruit spritzers, salsas, chutney, bruschetta and more! This unique appliance will make almost all of your grating and slicing a breeze.

To properly use your saladXPRESS™, follow the Owner's Manual carefully. The following tips will enhance your use of the saladXPRESS™:

❧ *One of the most important facts to remember when using your saladXPRESS™ is that the slicing and grating discs are sharp. The discs provide superior slicing and grating, however they must be handled carefully when attaching, using and removing the discs. Use caution while cleaning the discs to avoid injury.*

❧ *Always use the plunger when feeding food into the chute of the saladXPRESS™ bowl. This is especially important to avoid injury while the appliance is running.*

❧ *Various nuts and seeds that are especially hard may require more than one grating cycle to ensure uniform size and texture. If the nuts or seeds are not uniform after grating or slicing them once, simply remove them from the saladXPRESS™ bowl and feed them through the chute again.*

❧ *Use a plastic spatula to scrape down the sides of the saladXPRESS™ after grating or slicing very soft cheeses, butter, margarine or very ripe, soft fruit.*

❧ *The saladXPRESS™ is easy to use, however it should not be used by young children. Carefully supervise any children who use the saladXPRESS™.*

❧ *Use very fresh, ripe fruit, vegetables and other ingredients when preparing the recipes in this cookbook. Unripe fruit and vegetables do not offer the full flavor or nutritional value provided by fruit and vegetables that are used at their peak.*

- Look for firm, intensely-colored tomatoes, melons that have a pleasing and sweet aroma, peppers that are smooth and unwrinkled and mangos and papaya that are not soft, but yield to the touch.

- Always wash fruit and vegetables carefully before cutting or peeling. This helps eliminate bacteria from the outer rind or peel from transferring to the inner fruit or vegetable.

- If you are actively working to achieve a more healthful diet, you may substitute lowfat or reduced-fat foods for the ingredients in these recipes. Salad dressings can be made without any fat by increasing the juice or acid used and increasing the water to compensate.

- Use egg substitute as a healthy, no-fat alternative to whole eggs.

- The nutritional analyses provided for the recipes are offered as a guideline for each recipe. The actual analysis of each recipe may differ, depending on the ingredients you specifically select. For example, if you choose a lowfat mayonnaise in lieu of a nonfat mayonnaise, the resulting fat counts and calories will be a bit higher than those listed.

Chapter 1

Appetizers, Salsas & Beverages

Antipasto Ensalada

1/4 cup	extra virgin olive oil
2 tbsp.	balsamic vinegar
1 tbsp.	lemon juice
2 tsp.	prepared mustard
1/2 tsp.	sugar
1 clove	garlic, minced
1 tsp.	fresh basil, minced
1/2 tsp.	fresh oregano, minced
1/8 tsp.	salt
1 medium	cucumber, peeled
1 large	tomato
1	red bell pepper, seeded
2 cups	cauliflower florets
2 cups	romaine lettuce, torn
2	boneless, skinless, chicken breast halves, cooked and diced
8 oz.	dry salami, cubed
4 oz.	mozzarella cheese, cubed

In a small bowl, whisk together the oil, vinegar, lemon juice, mustard, sugar, garlic, basil, oregano and salt. Refrigerate for 1 hour.

Attach the slicing disc to the main body of the saladXPRESS™ and fasten it to the bowl, securing the safety latches. Use the slice/grate function and feed the cucumber through the food chute. Repeat the process with the tomato and bell pepper. Remove the bowl and add the cauliflower. Toss to blend. To serve, arrange the lettuce on a serving platter and top with the vegetables, chicken, salami and cheese. Drizzle the vinaigrette over the platter before serving.

❧ SERVES 8.

Calories:. 254	Carbohydrates: . . . . 6 g.
Total Fat: . . . . 20 g.	Protein: . . . . 15 g.
Saturated Fat:. . . . . 1 g.	Cholesterol: . . . . 18 mg.
% Calories from Fat: 68	Sodium: . . . . 622 mg.

Fresh Tomato & Basil Appetizer Pie

Potato Crust:

1/2 small	white onion
3	raw baking potatoes, peeled
1/2 tsp.	salt
1	egg, beaten
1 tbsp.	vegetable oil

Tomato & Basil Filling:

8	plum tomatoes, sliced
1/2 tsp.	salt
1/4 tsp.	ground black pepper
8 slices	turkey bacon, cooked crisp and crumbled
1 tbsp.	fresh basil, chopped
1 tbsp.	fresh Italian parsley, chopped
3/4 cup	Parmesan cheese, grated
1/3 cup	lowfat mayonnaise

Preheat the oven to 400°F. Attach the grating disc to the main body of the saladXPRESS™ and fasten it to the bowl, securing the safety latches. Use the slice/grate function and feed the onion through the chute. Remove the onion and repeat the process with the potatoes. Salt the potatoes and let them sit for 10 minutes. Spin dry the potatoes for 10 seconds to remove the excess water from the potatoes.

In a separate bowl, combine the potatoes, egg and onion. Pat into a 10-inch pie plate that has been coated with nonstick cooking spray. Bake for 35 to 40 minutes, or until the crust is golden brown. Brush the crust with oil after 20 minutes of baking to crisp it. Remove from the oven and reduce the heat to 350°F.

Use the saladXPRESS™ to slice the tomatoes into 1/4-inch thick slices. Layer half of the tomatoes onto the baked crust. Season the tomatoes with half of the salt and pepper. Sprinkle half of the bacon and half of the fresh herbs over the tomatoes. Repeat the layers. In a small bowl, combine the Parmesan cheese and mayonnaise. Carefully spread the cheese and mayonnaise over the top of the tomato layers. Bake, uncovered for 30 minutes, or until the cheese begins to brown.

SERVES 10.

Calories: *74*	*Carbohydrates:* . . . . *6 g.*
Total Fat:. . . . . *4 g.*	*Protein:* . . . . *4 g.*
Saturated Fat:. . . . . *1 g.*	*Cholesterol:* . . . . *29 mg.*
% Calories from Fat: *48*	*Sodium:* . . . . *408 mg.*

Pesto & Sweet Pepper Pizza

Toppings:

1	purple onion, peeled and quartered
1	sweet red bell pepper, seeded
1	green bell pepper, seeded
2 tbsp.	extra virgin olive oil, divided
1 tbsp.	water
2 tbsp.	cornmeal
1/4 cup	goat cheese
3/4 cup	mozzarella cheese, shredded
1/4 cup	Parmesan cheese, grated

Pesto:

2 cups	fresh basil leaves
2 cloves	garlic
3 tbsp.	pine nuts
1/4 cup	extra virgin olive oil
1/2 cup	Parmesan cheese, grated
1	12-inch prepackaged pizza round

Attach the slicing disc to the main body of the saladXPRESS™ and fasten it to the bowl, securing the safety latches. Use the slice/grate function and feed the onion through the food chute. Repeat the process with the red and green bell peppers. Remove the bowl and transfer the onion and bell peppers to a separate bowl. Set aside.

To prepare the pesto, use the grating disc and feed the basil, garlic and pine nuts through the food chute into the serving bowl, as directed above. Transfer the pesto into a small bowl and add the oil and Parmesan cheese. Mix thoroughly and refrigerate.

Sauté the onions and bell peppers over medium heat in 1 tablespoon of the olive oil and the water. When the bell peppers are soft, drain and set aside. Spread the remaining oil over a 12-inch pizza pan and sprinkle the cornmeal over the oil. Place the pizza round on the pan and spread the pesto evenly over the crust. Crumble the goat cheese evenly over the pesto. Add the onion, bell peppers and remaining cheeses. Bake for 15 minutes at 375°F until the crust is slightly brown.

~**~ SERVES 8.

Calories:. *447*	*Carbohydrates:* . . . . *41 g.*
Total Fat: . . . . *25 g.*	*Protein:* . . . . *20 g.*
Saturated Fat: . . . . *10 g.*	*Cholesterol:* . . . . *21 mg.*
% Calories from Fat: *48*	*Sodium:* . . . . *622 mg.*

Crimini Mushroom Crostini

8 oz.	nonfat cream cheese, softened
4 oz.	mild goat cheese
1/4 cup	nonfat milk
2 tbsp.	fresh chives, minced
	salt to taste
3 cups	crimini mushrooms, stems removed
2 cloves	garlic
1 tsp.	extra virgin olive oil
2 tbsp.	fresh flat-leaf parsley, minced
2 tsp.	fresh lemon juice
1/2 tsp.	freshly ground black pepper
1	large baguette, sliced into 1/4-inch rounds

In a medium bowl, combine the cream cheese, goat cheese, milk, chives and salt. Blend together well and set aside.

Attach the slicing disc to the main body of the saladXPRESS™ and fasten it to the bowl, securing the safety latches. Use the slice/grate function and feed the mushrooms and garlic into the food chute. Remove the bowl and transfer the mushrooms and garlic to a medium-sized skillet. Sauté in the olive oil until all the liquid is absorbed. Remove from the heat and mix in the parsley, lemon juice and black pepper.

Using the saladXPRESS™, slice the baguette. Assemble the crostini by placing the baguette slices on a large baking sheet. Spread each piece of bread with 1 tablespoon of the cheese blend. Top each with 1 tablespoon of the mushrooms and herbs. Broil for 3 minutes, or until the crostini are crisp and lightly browned on the edges.

✺ MAKES 20 CROSTINI.

Calories:. 110	Carbohydrates: . . . . 16 g.
Total Fat:. . . . . 2 g.	Protein:. . . . . 6 g.
Saturated Fat:. . . . . 1 g.	Cholesterol: . . . . 5 mg.
% Calories from Fat: 20	Sodium:. . . . . 272 mg.

Fresh Herb Bruschetta

2	Roma tomatoes, peeled and seeded
3 oz.	Parmesan cheese
6 slices	French bread, cut into 1/2-inch slices
1 sprig	fresh basil, finely chopped
1 tsp.	dried oregano
1 sprig	fresh thyme, finely chopped
1/4 tsp.	salt
1/4 tsp.	black pepper
6 tbsp.	extra virgin olive oil
2 cloves	garlic, minced

Attach the slicing disc to the main body of the saladXPRESS™ and fasten it to the bowl, securing the safety latches. Use the slice/grate function and feed the tomatoes through the food chute. Remove the tomatoes to a separate bowl. Replace the slicing disc with the grating disc and grate the Parmesan cheese.

Place the bread on a baking sheet and broil for 3 minutes, or until crispy. Layer the tomatoes on the toast and sprinkle each piece with the basil, oregano and thyme. Season with salt and pepper. Drizzle the olive oil and garlic over each bruschetta and top with the Parmesan cheese. Place back into the oven to warm. Serve immediately.

~& MAKES 6 SERVINGS.

Calories:. 283	Carbohydrates: . . . . 18 g.
Total Fat: . . . . 19 g.	Protein: . . . . 9 g.
Saturated Fat:. . . . . 5 g.	Cholesterol: . . . . 6 mg.
% Calories from Fat: 61	Sodium: . . . . 507 mg.

Romano & Rosemary Bruschetta

4 oz.	Romano cheese
1 cup	walnuts, halved
1/4 tsp.	salt
2 tbsp.	extra virgin olive oil, divided
1 sprig	rosemary, finely minced
1	baguette, sliced horizontally, and then into 4-inch pieces

Attach the grating disc to the main body of the saladXPRESS™ and fasten it to the bowl, securing the safety latches. Use the slice/grate function and feed the Romano cheese through the chute. Repeat the process with the walnuts. Remove the bowl and add the salt and 1 tablespoon of oil to the cheese and walnuts. Mix together well.

Place the sliced baguette on a baking sheet and brush the top of each with the remaining oil. Toast under the broiler for 30 seconds. Remove and spread the cheese and walnuts over the top of each slice. Return the bruschetta to the broiler for another 30 seconds, or until the cheese is melted. Serve immediately.

MAKES 16 SLICES.

Calories:. 172	Carbohydrates: . . . . 18 g.
Total Fat:. . . . . 9 g.	Protein:. . . . . 6 g.
Saturated Fat:. . . . . 2 g.	Cholesterol: . . . . 7 mg.
% Calories from Fat: 45	Sodium: . . . . 316 mg.

Mozzarella & Oregano Bruschetta

3	Roma tomatoes, peeled and seeded
1/2 small	red onion
2 tbsp.	fresh oregano
1/4 lb.	mozzarella
2 tbsp.	balsamic vinegar
2 tbsp.	extra virgin olive oil
	salt and pepper
4 slices	toasted Italian bread

Attach the slicing disc to the main body of the saladXPRESS™ and fasten it to the bowl, securing the safety latches. Use the slice/grate function and feed the tomatoes through the food chute. Repeat the process with the red onion. Attach the grating disc to the main body of the bowl and feed the oregano and mozzarella through the food chute. Remove the bowl and add the vinegar and oil to the vegetables and cheese. Stir together well and season with salt and pepper to taste. Top the toasted bread with the mixture and place on a baking sheet. Broil until the cheese melts. Serve immediately.

SERVES 4.

Calories:. 240	Carbohydrates: . . . . 20 g.
Total Fat: . . . . 13 g.	Protein: . . . . 11 g.
Saturated Fat:. . . . . 4 g.	Cholesterol: . . . . 15 mg.
% Calories from Fat: 49	Sodium: . . . . 316 mg.

Italian Pepper Bruschetta

1 small	red bell pepper, seeded
1 small	green bell pepper, seeded
1 small	yellow bell pepper, seeded
1 small	orange bell pepper, seeded
1/2 small	red onion, quartered
2 cloves	garlic, finely minced
1/4 cup	fresh basil leaves, minced
1 tsp.	black pepper
1 tbsp.	extra virgin olive oil
1 small	sourdough bread baguette, sliced into thin rounds

Attach the slicing disc to the main body of the saladXPRESS™ and fasten it to the bowl, securing the safety latches. Use the slice/grate function and feed the red bell pepper through the chute. Repeat the process with the remaining bell peppers and onion. Remove the bowl and add the garlic, basil, black pepper and olive oil.

Assemble the bread rounds on a baking sheet and top each slice with 1 tablespoon of the bruschetta vegetables. Broil in the oven for 5 minutes, or until the bread is toasted and golden brown.

SERVES 20.

Calories: 92	Carbohydrates: . . . . 16 g.
Total Fat: . . . . 2 g.	Protein: . . . . 3 g.
Saturated Fat: . . . . <1 g.	Cholesterol: . . . . 0 mg.
% Calories from Fat: 16	Sodium: . . . . 173 mg.

Peach & Sweet Pepper Chutney

3	ripe peaches, peeled and pitted
1	red bell pepper, seeded
1	green bell pepper, seeded
1 small	jalapeño pepper, seeded
2 tsp.	fresh lime juice
1 tbsp.	brown sugar, packed
1/2 tsp.	ground coriander
1/4 cup	golden raisins

Attach the grating disc to the main body of the saladXPRESS™ and fasten it to the bowl, securing the safety latches. Use the slice/grate function and feed the peaches through the food chute. Repeat the process with the bell peppers and the jalapeño. Remove the bowl and add the lime juice, brown sugar and the coriander. Mix until well blended. Place the chutney in a serving bowl and add the raisins, mixing lightly. Refrigerate for at least 6 hours to allow the flavors to marry.

SERVES 15.

Calories: 25	Carbohydrates: . . . . 6 g.
Total Fat: . . . . <1 g.	Protein: . . . . <1 g.
Saturated Fat: . . . . <1 g.	Cholesterol: . . . . 0 mg.
% Calories from Fat: 3	Sodium: . . . . 20 mg.

Black Bean & Mango Chutney

1	mango, peeled and seeded
4	green onions
1/2 small	purple onion, quartered
1	jalapeño chile, seeded
1 small	red bell pepper, seeded
1	lime, peeled and halved
1 small	tangerine, peeled and seeds removed
1/4 cup	black beans, rinsed and drained
1 tsp.	ground ginger
1 tsp.	fresh oregano, snipped
1 tbsp.	rice vinegar
1 tbsp.	extra virgin olive oil
1 tsp.	ground cumin

Attach the grating disc to the main body of the saladXPRESS™ and fasten it to the bowl, securing the safety latches. Use the slice/grate function and feed the mango through the chute. Repeat the process with onions, jalapeño, red bell pepper, lime and tangerine. Remove the bowl and add the remaining ingredients. Mix well and adjust the seasoning to taste. Let stand at room temperature for 2 hours before serving.

✦ SERVES 10.

Calories: 47	Carbohydrates: . . . . 8 g.
Total Fat: . . . . 2 g.	Protein: . . . . <1 g.
Saturated Fat: . . . . <1 g.	Cholesterol: . . . . 0 mg.
% Calories from Fat: 30	Sodium: . . . . 63 mg.

Spicy Pear & Apple Chutney

1 small	sweet onion, peeled and quartered
1 small	seedless tangelo, peeled
2 small	pears, cored
1 large	tart apple, peeled and cored
1 1/2 cups	cider vinegar
1/4 cup	water
1 tbsp.	ground ginger
1/2 tsp.	salt
1 tsp.	ground cinnamon
1 clove	garlic, peeled
2 cups	brown sugar, firmly packed
1 cup	fresh cranberries, washed
2 tbsp.	almonds, blanched and slivered

Attach the grating disc to the main body of the saladXPRESS™ and fasten it to the bowl, securing the safety latches. Use the slice/grate function and feed the onion and the tangelo through the chute. Remove the bowl and transfer the onion and tangelo to a separate bowl. Set aside. Remove the grating disc and replace it with the slicing disc. Slice the pears and apple and set aside.

In a medium saucepan, combine vinegar, onion, tangelo, water, ginger, salt, cinnamon and garlic. Cook over medium-high heat and bring to a boil, stirring frequently. Reduce the heat to low and cook for 15 minutes, stirring occasionally. Add the brown sugar, pears, apple, cranberries and almonds and stir until the sugar dissolves. Cook until the fruit is soft and the liquid thickens slightly, stirring occasionally for about 1 hour. Cool to room temperature, cover and refrigerate.

SERVES 24.

Calories: 93	Carbohydrates: . . . . 24 g.
Total Fat:. . . . . 1 g.	Protein: . . . . <1 g.
Saturated Fat:. . . . . <1 g.	Cholesterol: . . . . 0 mg.
% Calories from Fat: 2	Sodium:. . . . . 56 mg.

Sun-Dried Tomato & Chile Salsa

2 cups	sundried tomatoes, whole
1 small	red onion, peeled and quartered
2 cloves	garlic, peeled
2 small	green chilies, seeded
4 sprigs	fresh cilantro
1 tbsp.	fresh lime juice
3 tbsp.	fresh tomato juice
2 tsp.	chili powder
1 tsp.	ground black pepper
1/2 tsp.	salt

Attach the grating disc to the main body of the saladXPRESS™ and fasten it to the bowl, securing the safety latches. Use the slice/grate function and feed the tomatoes through the chute. Repeat the process with the red onion, garlic, chilies and cilantro. Remove the bowl and add the lime juice, tomato juice, chili powder, black pepper and salt. Toss gently, cover and refrigerate for at least 2 hours. Serve fresh.

~ SERVES 10.

Calories: 40		Carbohydrates: . . . . 9 g.	
Total Fat: . . . . <1 g.		Protein: . . . . 2 g.	
Saturated Fat: . . . . <1 g.		Cholesterol: . . . . 0 mg.	
% Calories from Fat: 9		Sodium: . . . . 350 mg.	

Zesty Jicama & Orange Salsa

1 1/2 cups	jicama, peeled and roughly chopped
1 medium	orange, peeled and seeded
1	jalapeño pepper, seeded
3 sprigs	fresh parsley
1 tbsp.	white vinegar
1/2 tsp.	ground black pepper
1/2 tsp.	salt

Attach the grating disc to the main body of the saladXPRESS™ and fasten it to the bowl, securing the safety latches. Use the slice/grate function and feed the jicama through the chute. Repeat the process with the orange, pepper and parsley sprigs. Remove the bowl and add the vinegar, pepper and salt. Stir gently to blend. Cover and refrigerate for up to 2 days.

MAKES 10 TO 12 SERVINGS.

Calories: 12	Carbohydrates: . . . . 3 g.
Total Fat: . . . . <1 g.	Protein: . . . . <1 g.
Saturated Fat: . . . . <1 g.	Cholesterol: . . . . 0 mg.
% Calories from Fat: 3	Sodium: . . . . 128 mg.

Chile Verde Salsa

1 1/2 cups	tomatillos, seeded
1/2 small	white onion, peeled and quartered
1	serrano chile, seeded
3 sprigs	fresh cilantro
4 sprigs	fresh parsley
3 cloves	garlic, peeled
1/2 tsp.	salt
1 tsp.	black pepper
1/2 tsp.	crushed red pepper
2 tbsp.	white vinegar
2 tbsp.	water

Attach the grating disc to the main body of the saladXPRESS™ and fasten it to the bowl, securing the safety latches. Use the slice/grate function and feed the tomatillos through the chute. Repeat the process with the onion, chile, cilantro, parsley and garlic. Remove the bowl and add the salt, pepper, red pepper, vinegar and water. Blend well and let stand for at least 1 hour.

∿ MAKES 12 TO 16 SERVINGS.

Calories: 7	Carbohydrates: . . . . 1 g.
Total Fat: . . . . <1 g.	Protein: . . . . <1 g.
Saturated Fat: . . . . <1 g.	Cholesterol: . . . . 0 mg.
% Calories from Fat: 16	Sodium: . . . . 128 mg.

Fresh Peach Salsa

1/2	pineapple, peeled
2	peaches, peeled and pitted
2	green onions
2 sprigs	fresh parsley
1 clove	garlic, peeled
2 tbsp.	pineapple juice
1/4 cup	white vinegar
1/4 cup	honey
1/2 tsp.	salt

Attach the grating disc to the main body of the saladXPRESS™ and fasten it to the bowl, securing the safety latches. Use the slice/grate function and feed the pineapple through the chute. Repeat the process with the peaches, onions, parsley and garlic. Remove the bowl and add the pineapple juice, vinegar, honey and salt. Gently stir the mixture to blend well. Cover and refrigerate for at least 2 hours.

SERVES 10.

Calories: 53	Carbohydrates: . . . . 13 g.
Total Fat: . . . . <1 g.	Protein: . . . . <1 g.
Saturated Fat: . . . . <1 g.	Cholesterol: . . . . 0 mg.
% Calories from Fat: 2	Sodium: . . . . 118 mg.

Colorful Garden Salsa

1 lb.	plum tomatoes, seeded
1/2 small	white onion, halved
2 ribs	celery, cut in 2-inch lengths
1 small	green bell pepper, seeded
1 small	yellow bell pepper, seeded
1 small	orange bell pepper, seeded
1/2	cucumber, peeled
5 sprigs	fresh basil
2 sprigs	fresh parsley
2 cloves	garlic, peeled
2 tbsp.	extra-virgin olive oil
3 tbsp.	balsamic vinegar
1 tbsp.	Dijon mustard
1/2 tsp.	black pepper

Attach the grating disc to the main body of the saladXPRESS™ and fasten it to the bowl, securing the safety latches. Use the slice/grate function and feed the tomatoes through the chute. Repeat the process with the onion, celery, bell peppers, cucumber, basil, parsley and garlic.

Remove the bowl and add the oil, vinegar, mustard and pepper. Toss gently to blend. Cover and refrigerate for 2 hours until the flavors have combined.

❧ MAKES 14 SERVINGS

Calories: 37		Carbohydrates: . . . . 4 g.	
Total Fat: . . . . 2 g.		Protein: . . . . <1 g.	
Saturated Fat: . . . . <1 g.		Cholesterol: . . . . <1 mg.	
% Calories from Fat: 52		Sodium: . . . . 18 mg.	

Tex-Mex Salsa

2 slices	turkey bacon, cooked
1/2 small	red onion, halved
2 cloves	garlic, peeled
1 medium	green bell pepper
4 sprigs	fresh parsley
1 large	tomato, peeled and seeded
2 cups	canned black-eyed peas, drained
2 tbsp.	extra virgin olive oil
1/4 cup	tomato juice
2 tbsp.	water
1/2 tsp.	crushed red pepper
1 tsp.	ground black pepper

Attach the grating disc to the main body of the saladXPRESS™ and fasten it to the bowl, securing the safety latches. Use the slice/grate function and feed the bacon through the chute. Repeat the process with the onion, garlic, green pepper, parsley and tomato. Set aside.

Lightly spray a medium saucepan with cooking spray and sauté the grated vegetables and bacon until tender, about 5 minutes. Add the peas, oil, tomato juice, water, red pepper and the black pepper. Cook for another 3 minutes. Reduce the heat and simmer over low heat for 10 minutes. Serve warm or chilled.

✒ SERVES 12 TO 16.

Calories: 53	Carbohydrates: . . . . 6 g.
Total Fat: . . . . 2 g.	Protein: . . . . 2 g.
Saturated Fat: . . . . <1 g.	Cholesterol: . . . . 1 mg.
% Calories from Fat: 37	Sodium: . . . . 141 mg.

Black Soybean & Cilantro Salsa

1	ripe tomato
1/2 small	white onion
1 small	green bell pepper, seeded
4 sprigs	fresh parsley
2 sprigs	fresh cilantro
1 clove	garlic
16 oz.	can black soybeans, rinsed and drained
9 oz.	frozen corn kernels, thawed and drained
1/4 cup	balsamic vinegar
2 tsp.	hot sauce
1 tsp.	chili powder
1/2 tsp.	ground black pepper
1/2 tsp.	salt
1/4 cup	canola oil

Attach the grating disc to the main body of the saladXPRESS™ and fasten it to the bowl, securing the safety latches. Use the slice/grate function and feed the tomato through the chute. Repeat the process with the onion, bell pepper, parsley, cilantro and garlic. Remove the bowl and add the beans and corn. Mix to blend.

In a separate bowl, whisk together the vinegar, hot sauce, chili powder, black pepper, salt and oil. Add the bean salsa and blend thoroughly. Cover and refrigerate for at least 2 hours before serving.

❧ SERVES 20.

Calories: 63	Carbohydrates: . . . . 5 g.
Total Fat: . . . . 4 g.	Protein: . . . . 3 g.
Saturated Fat: . . . . <1 g.	Cholesterol: . . . . 0 mg.
% Calories from Fat: 53	Sodium: . . . . 70 mg.

Sweet Coconut & Papaya Salsa

1	ripe papaya, peeled and seeded
1	ripe mango, peeled and seeded
1/4 small	coconut, husked and roughly chopped
2 sprigs	fresh cilantro
1/2 cup	pineapple juice
2 tsp.	crushed red pepper
1 tbsp.	white vinegar

Attach the grating disc to the main body of the saladXPRESS™ and fasten it to the bowl, securing the safety latches. Use the slice/grate function and feed the papaya through the chute. Repeat the process with the mango, coconut and cilantro. Remove the bowl and add the pineapple juice, red pepper and vinegar. Toss gently to combine thoroughly. Cover and refrigerate for at least 2 hours before serving.

SERVES 10.

Calories:	62	Carbohydrates:	11 g.
Total Fat:	2 g.	Protein:	<1 g.
Saturated Fat:	2 g.	Cholesterol:	0 mg.
% Calories from Fat:	29	Sodium:	21 mg.

Rio Grande Salsa

1 medium	red onion, peeled and quartered
2 sprigs	fresh rosemary
1 sprig	fresh parsley
2 tsp.	extra-virgin olive oil
1 tsp.	sugar
2 tsp.	red vinegar
1/4 tsp.	ground black pepper
1/4 tsp.	salt

Attach the grating disc to the main body of the saladXPRESS™ and fasten it to the bowl, securing the safety latches. Use the slice/grate function and feed the onion through the chute. Remove the bowl and transfer the onions to a separate bowl. Repeat the process with the rosemary and parsley and set aside.

Over medium-high heat, sauté the red onions in the olive oil until they are lightly browned. Reduce the heat to medium and add the sugar, red vinegar, rosemary, parsley, black pepper and salt. Simmer, stirring occasionally, for 5 minutes. Serve warm or at room temperature.

SERVES 4 TO 5.

Calories: 30		Carbohydrates: . . . . 3 g.	
Total Fat: . . . . 2 g.		Protein: . . . . <1 g.	
Saturated Fat: . . . . <1 g.		Cholesterol: . . . . 0 mg.	
% Calories from Fat: 58		Sodium: . . . . 117 mg.	

Rainbow Fruit Spritzer

1	tart apple, cored
1/2	pineapple
1 cup	green grapes
2 cups	pineapple juice
2 cups	white grape juice
1/4 cup	lime juice
750 ml.	unsweetened apple juice
12 oz.	can ginger ale

Attach the slicing disc to the main body of the saladXPRESS™ and fasten it to the bowl, securing the safety latches. Use the slice/grate function and feed the apple through the chute. Repeat the process with the pineapple and grapes. Transfer the fruit to a large pitcher. Add the pineapple juice, grape juice, lime juice, apple juice and ginger ale. Stir gently and refrigerate for 1 hour before serving.

SERVES 10.

Calories:. 145	Carbohydrates: . . . . 25 g.
Total Fat: . . . . <1 g.	Protein: . . . . <1 g.
Saturated Fat:. . . . . <1 g.	Cholesterol: . . . . 0 mg.
% Calories from Fat: 1	Sodium:. . . . . 14 mg.

Lime & Kiwi Chiller

1	kiwi, peeled
2	oranges, peeled and sectioned
2	lemons, peeled and halved
2	limes, peeled and halved
1/4 cup	white grape juice
1/2 fl. oz.	grenadine-flavored syrup
2 tsp.	lime juice
1 tbsp.	sugar or sugar substitute
28 oz.	club soda, chilled

Attach the slicing disc to the main body of the saladXPRESS™and fasten it to the bowl, securing the safety latches. Use the slice/grate function and feed the kiwi through the chute. Transfer the sliced kiwi to a small bowl, reattach the slicing disc and repeat the process with the oranges, lemons and limes.

In a large pitcher, combine the sliced oranges, lemons, limes, white grape juice, grenadine syrup, lime juice and sugar. Mix well and refrigerate overnight. Just before serving, add the club soda and sliced kiwi.

❧ SERVES 8.

Calories: 84	Carbohydrates: . . . . 18 g.
Total Fat: . . . . <1 g.	Protein: . . . . <1 g.
Saturated Fat: . . . . <1 g.	Cholesterol: . . . . 0 mg.
% Calories from Fat: 2	Sodium: . . . . 23 mg.

Tart & Tangy Citrus Cooler

2	oranges, peeled and sectioned
1	lemon, peeled and halved
1	lime, peeled and halved
1	red apple, peeled and cored
1	pear, peeled and cored
1/2 gal.	cranberry juice
1 cup	orange juice
2 tsp.	orange extract
1/2 cup	white grape juice
2 tbsp.	fresh mint, minced
16 oz.	pkg. frozen peaches, sliced
28 oz.	club soda

Attach the slicing disc to the main body of the saladXPRESS™ and fasten it to the bowl, securing the safety latches. Use the slice/grate function and feed the oranges through the chute. Repeat the process with the lemon, lime, apple and pear. Remove the bowl and transfer the fruit to a large container. Add the cranberry juice, orange juice, orange extract, white grape juice and mint. Cover and refrigerate for at least 12 hours.

To serve, fill a clear glass pitcher with the juice, adding the frozen peaches. Pour into chilled glasses with a splash of club soda.

SERVES 12 TO 16.

Calories:	170	Carbohydrates:	12 g.
Total Fat:	<1 g.	Protein:	<1 g.
Saturated Fat:	<1 g.	Cholesterol:	0 mg.
% Calories from Fat:	<1	Sodium:	17 mg.

Tropical Island Punch

2	tart apples, peeled and cored
2	oranges, peeled and sectioned
1	pineapple, peeled, halved and cored
1	lime, peeled and halved
1 cup	grape juice
1/2 cup	coconut-flavored syrup
1 tbsp.	rum flavoring
1 cup	apple juice
1 cup	orange juice
2 tbsp.	sugar
28 oz.	bottle seltzer

Attach the slicing disc to the main body of the saladXPRESS™ and fasten it to the bowl, securing the safety latches. Use the slice/grate function and feed the apples through the chute. Repeat the process with the oranges, pineapple and lime. Remove the bowl and place the fruit in a large plastic or glass container. Add the grape juice, coconut syrup, rum flavoring, apple juice, orange juice and sugar. Mix well and refrigerate for 24 hours. Before serving, add the club soda.

❧ MAKES 10 TO 12 SERVINGS.

Calories:. 191	Carbohydrates: . . . . 28 g.
Total Fat: . . . . <1 g.	Protein: . . . . <1 g.
Saturated Fat:. . . . . <1 g.	Cholesterol: . . . . 0 mg.
% Calories from Fat: 1	Sodium:. . . . . 9 mg.

Raspberry & Orange Summer Delight

1	orange, peeled and sectioned
1	lemon, peeled and halved
750 ml.	apple juice
2 tsp.	orange extract
1 tbsp.	sugar
8 small	clusters of green grapes
6 oz.	pkg. frozen raspberries

Attach the slicing disc to the main body of the saladXPRESS™ and fasten it to the bowl, securing the safety latches. Use the slice/grate function and feed the orange and lemon through the chute. Remove the bowl and set aside.

In a large pitcher, combine apple juice, orange extract, sugar, orange and lemon. Blend well and refrigerate for 1 hour. To serve, pour the punch into 8 glasses. Place a cluster of grapes in each glass along with a few raspberries.

SERVES 8.

Calories:. 116	Carbohydrates: . . . . 13 g.
Total Fat: . . . . <1 g.	Protein: . . . . <1 g.
Saturated Fat:. . . . . <1 g.	Cholesterol: . . . . 0 mg.
% Calories from Fat: 2	Sodium:. . . . . 7 mg.

Chapter 2

Entrées &
Main Dish
Salads

Sautéed Scallops with Spinach & Broccoli Sprouts

2 tbsp.	vegetable oil, divided
1 lb.	scallops, cleaned and dried
2 tsp.	Dijon mustard
1 1/2 tbsp.	balsamic vinegar
4	green onions
2	carrots, peeled
2 bunches	spinach leaves, cleaned
1 cup	corn kernels
1 bunch	broccoli sprouts for garnish

In a large skillet, heat 1 tablespoon of the oil over medium-high heat and sauté the scallops until they are golden and cooked through. With a slotted spoon, transfer the scallops to a bowl and cover to keep warm. In a small bowl, whisk together the mustard, vinegar and the remaining oil. Add to the scallops and toss gently.

Attach the grating disc to the main body of the saladXPRESS™ and fasten it to the bowl, securing the safety latches. Use the slice/grate function and feed the onions through the chute. Repeat the process with the carrots and the spinach. Remove the bowl and add the corn. Mix together well. To serve, divide the vegetables between 4 dinner plates, and top with equal portions of the scallops. Garnish with the sprouts.

❧ SERVES 4.

Calories:. 261	Carbohydrates: . . . . 22 g.
Total Fat:. . . . . 9 g.	Protein: . . . . 26 g.
Saturated Fat:. . . . . 1 g.	Cholesterol: . . . . 37 mg.
% Calories from Fat: 29	Sodium: . . . . 437 mg.

Malaysian Sweet & Sour Chicken Vegetable Bowls

2	boneless, skinless chicken breasts, cooked
2	carrots, peeled
1	red bell pepper
1/2 lb.	broccoli, tough stems removed
2 cloves	garlic
1 tbsp.	vegetable oil
1 tsp.	crushed red chile pepper
1/2 tsp.	ground turmeric
1/4 cup	white vinegar
1/4 cup	water
1 tbsp.	sugar
1/2 cup	salted roasted peanuts, finely chopped
4 cups	steamed long grain white rice

Attach the slicing disc to the main body of the saladXPRESS™ and fasten it to the bowl, securing the safety latches. Use the slice/grate function and feed the chicken through the chute. Repeat the process with the carrots, red bell pepper, broccoli and garlic.

In a skillet over medium-low heat, sauté the red chile pepper in the oil. Add the sliced vegetables and chicken, cooking for 3 minutes. Add the turmeric and cook and stir for 2 minutes. Add the vinegar, water and sugar and increase the heat to high. When the liquid begins to boil and the vegetables are crisp-tender, stir in the peanuts. Remove from the heat. Serve over individual bowls of rice.

SERVES 4 TO 5.

Calories:. 350	Carbohydrates: . . . . 48 g.
Total Fat: . . . . 11 g.	Protein: . . . . 16 g.
Saturated Fat:. . . . . 4 g.	Cholesterol: . . . . 16 mg.
% Calories from Fat: 28	Sodium: . . . . 106 mg.

Fiery Chile Shrimp & Vegetables over Polenta

1	serrano chile, seeded
1 small	tomato, seeded
1/2 small	white onion, peeled
2 cloves	garlic
2 tbsp.	fresh cilantro
1 small	jicama, peeled and roughly cut
2 tbsp.	sesame oil
2 tbsp.	rice vinegar
1/2 cup	water
	salt and pepper to taste
1 cup	canned corn kernels, drained
1 large	tomato, roughly chopped
18 medium	cooked shrimp, deveined and tails removed
1 lb.	prepared polenta, sliced into 1-inch rounds

Attach the grating disc to the main body of the saladXPRESS™ and fasten it to the bowl, securing the safety latches. Use the slice/grate function and feed the chile through the chute. Repeat the process with the small tomato, onion, garlic, cilantro and jicama. Remove the bowl and add the oil, vinegar and water. Blend well and add salt and pepper to taste. Spoon into a mixing bowl. Add the corn, large tomato and shrimp. Place the polenta rounds on a baking sheet and broil until slightly browned. To serve, arrange the polenta on individual plates and spoon the shrimp and vegetables over each plate.

Calories: *378*	*Carbohydrates:* . . . . *73 g.*
Total Fat: . . . . *7 g.*	*Protein:* . . . . *12 g.*
Saturated Fat: . . . . *<1 g.*	*Cholesterol:* . . . . *32 mg.*
% Calories from Fat: *16*	*Sodium:* . . . . *123 mg.*

Balsamic Dijon Chicken & Vegetable Kebabs

2 medium	zucchini, cleaned and ends removed
2 medium	crookneck squash, cleaned and ends removed
1 cup	balsamic vinegar
2 tbsp.	Dijon mustard
1 tbsp.	fresh parsley, minced
1 tbsp.	fresh thyme, minced
1/4 tsp.	fresh ground black pepper
1 lb.	boneless, skinless chicken breasts, cut into chunks
8	10-inch wooden skewers, soaked in water

Attach the slicing disc to the main body of the saladXPRESS™ and fasten it to the bowl, securing the safety latches. Use the slice/grate function and feed the zucchini and crookneck squash through the chute. Slice the squash into 1/2-inch thick pieces. In a sealable plastic bag combine the vinegar, mustard, parsley, thyme and black pepper. Add the squash and refrigerate for 1 hour or up to 12 hours.

Alternately thread the chicken and marinated vegetables on the 8 skewers and place the skewers on an indoor or outdoor grill. Grill, occasionally brushing the kebabs with the marinade for 20 to 30 minutes, or until the chicken is completely cooked and no pink remains. The vegetables will be just tender when ready to serve.

꙳ SERVES 4.

Calories:. 255	*Carbohydrates: . . . . 26 g.*
Total Fat:. . . . . 3 g.	*Protein: . . . . 33 g.*
Saturated Fat:. . . . . <1 g.	*Cholesterol: . . . . 66 mg.*
% Calories from Fat: 10	*Sodium: . . . . 133 mg.*

Shanghai Pork with Snow Peas & Sweet Onion

1/4 lb.	snow pea pods, trimmed and blanched
1 medium	carrot, peeled
1	red bell pepper
1	sweet Maui onion, peeled and quartered
1 lb.	pork loin, cooked and visible fat removed
3 cups	long grain white rice, steamed
1/4 cup	chicken broth
3 tbsp.	rice vinegar
3 tbsp.	low sodium soy sauce
1 tsp.	sesame oil
2 tbsp.	sesame seeds, toasted

Attach the slicing disc to the main body of the saladXPRESS™ and fasten it to the bowl, securing the safety latches. Use the slice/grate function and feed the snow peas through the chute. Repeat the process with the carrot, bell pepper, onion and pork.

Coat a large wok or sauté pan with nonstick cooking spray and add the pork and vegetables and the rice. Toss and sauté for 2 minutes. Add the chicken broth, vinegar, soy sauce and sesame oil. Sauté again until heated throughout. Serve topped with the sesame seeds.

SERVES 6.

Calories:. 319		Carbohydrates: . . . . 31 g.	
Total Fat:. . . . . 9 g.		Protein: . . . . 27 g.	
Saturated Fat:. . . . . 3 g.		Cholesterol: . . . . 64 mg.	
% Calories from Fat: 18		Sodium: . . . . 363 mg.	

Grilled Salmon & Vegetables in Lemon-Garlic Vinaigrette

2	zucchini, cleaned and ends removed
1 small	red onion, peeled and quartered
4 small	red potatoes, cleaned and quartered
1 lb.	salmon fillets, cut into 4 pieces

Lemon-Garlic Vinaigrette:

2	green onions
2 sprigs	parsley
1 clove	garlic
1/4 cup	extra virgin olive oil
2 tbsp.	rice vinegar
2 tbsp.	fresh lemon juice
1/2 tsp.	lemon zest
1/4 tsp.	black pepper

Attach the slicing disc to the main body of the saladXPRESS™ and fasten it to the bowl, securing the safety latches. Use the slice/grate function and feed the zucchini through the chute. Repeat the process with the onion and potatoes. Arrange 4 large squares of aluminum foil on a flat surface. Cover each piece with an additional layer of foil. Place equal portions of the vegetables on each square and top each with a salmon fillet.

Attach the grating disc to the main body of the saladXPRESS™ and fasten it to the bowl, securing the safety latches. Use the slice/grate function and feed the green onions, parsley and garlic through the chute. Place in a small bowl and add the oil, vinegar, lemon juice, zest and pepper. Shake or blend well. Pour the dressing over each portion of fish and vegetables and fold the foil edges securely together to form 4 pockets. Grill the salmon pockets over medium-hot coals until the salmon flakes easily with a fork and the vegetables are tender, about 20 to 25 minutes.

SERVES 4.

Calories:. 406	Carbohydrates: . . . . 15 g.
Total Fat: . . . . 18 g.	Protein: . . . . 26 g.
Saturated Fat:. . . . . 5 g.	Cholesterol: . . . . 74 mg.
% Calories from Fat: 49	Sodium: . . . . 241 mg.

Curried Lamb & Brown Rice

1/4	sweet onion
2 cups	white button mushrooms, cleaned and stems removed
1 rib	celery
1/2 tsp.	curry powder
1 tsp.	lime juice
1/2 tsp.	lime zest
1 tsp.	sugar
1 tsp.	vegetable oil
1 lb.	boneless lamb loin chops
1/2 cup	nonfat plain yogurt
1/4 cup	cashews, chopped
3 cups	brown rice, steamed
3	kiwis, peeled, for garnish

Attach the slicing disc to the main body of the saladXPRESS™ and fasten it to the bowl, securing the safety latches. Use the slice/grate function and feed the onion through the chute. Repeat the process with the mushrooms and celery. Remove the bowl and add the curry powder, lime juice, zest and sugar. Toss to combine.

In a large sauté pan over medium-high heat, sauté the lamb in the oil until it is cooked to medium, about 6 minutes. Add the vegetables and seasonings and sauté for 3 to 4 minutes, or until warmed through. Add the yogurt, stirring gently over medium heat until well-blended and warm. Add the cashews. To serve, place the brown rice on a serving platter and spoon the curried lamb and sauce over the top. Slice the kiwis in the saladXPRESS™ as directed above and garnish with the kiwis.

⮞ SERVES 6.

Calories: *298*	*Carbohydrates:* . . . . *35 g.*
Total Fat: . . . . *8 g.*	*Protein:* . . . . *21 g.*
Saturated Fat: . . . . *2 g.*	*Cholesterol:* . . . . *49 mg.*
% Calories from Fat: *17*	*Sodium:* . . . . *115 mg.*

Hong Kong Garlic Chicken Pizza

4	green onions
3 cloves	garlic
2 tbsp.	rice vinegar
2 tbsp.	low sodium soy sauce
2 tbsp.	sesame oil, divided
1/2 tsp.	crushed red pepper
1/4 tsp.	black pepper
12 oz.	boneless, skinless, chicken breast halves
1 tbsp.	cornstarch
4 oz.	reduced fat Monterey Jack cheese
4 oz.	reduced fat mozzarella cheese
1	12-inch round Italian flat bread
	slivered almonds for garnish

Attach the slicing disc to the main body of the saladXPRESS™ and fasten it to the bowl, securing the safety latches. Use the slice/grate function and feed the onions through the chute. Repeat the process with the garlic.

In a sealable plastic bag, combine half of the green onions, the garlic, rice vinegar, soy sauce, 1 tablespoon of the oil, red pepper and the black pepper. Add the chicken and turn to coat with the marinade. Refrigerate for 30 minutes. Drain the chicken and reserve the marinade. In a large skillet, heat the remaining oil and cook the chicken completely until no pink remains. Stir the cornstarch into the reserved marinade and add it to the skillet. Bring the sauce to a boil and cook for 5 minutes. Remove the skillet from the heat and cool slightly.

Attach the grating disc to the main body of the saladXPRESS™ and fasten it to the bowl, securing the safety latches. Use the slice/grate function and feed both of the cheeses through the chute. Set aside. Attach the slicing disc and slice the cooled chicken.

To assemble, place the flat bread on a baking sheet. Evenly place the chicken slices on the bread. Spoon the marinade sauce over the chicken. Layer the cheeses evenly over all. Bake the pizza at 375°F for 15 to 20 minutes until the cheese is bubbly and the pizza is hot throughout. Just before serving, top with the remaining onions and almonds.

SERVES 4 TO 6.

Calories:. 340	Carbohydrates: . . . . 38 g.
Total Fat: . . . . 14 g.	Protein: . . . . 27 g.
Saturated Fat: . . . . <1 g.	Cholesterol: . . . . 60 mg.
% Calories from Fat: 32	Sodium: . . . . 736 mg.

Mexican Jack Cheese & Refried Bean Pizza

2 cups	reduced fat Monterey Jack cheese
3	plum tomatoes
1	green bell pepper, seeded
4	green onions
1/4 cup	fresh cilantro, sliced
2 cloves	garlic, sliced
4 small	Italian flat breads
15 oz.	can refried beans
1/4 cup	Sun-Dried Tomato & Chile Salsa (see p. 28)

Attach the grating disc to the main body of the saladXPRESS™ and fasten it to the bowl, securing the safety latches. Use the slice/grate function and feed the cheese through the chute. Remove the cheese from the bowl and set aside. Using the slicing disc, slice the tomatoes, green bell pepper, onions, cilantro and garlic. Remove the bowl and set aside.

Preheat the oven to 400°F. Place the flatbreads on a baking sheet. Spread 1/4 of the beans on each flat bread. Cover the beans with 1/2 cup of the Jack cheese. Scatter the vegetables, cilantro and garlic evenly over each pizza. Bake for 15 minutes, or until the cheese has melted and each pizza is hot throughout. Drizzle the Sun-Dried Tomato & Chile Salsa over the top of the baked pizzas and serve immediately.

🍃 SERVES 4.

Calories:. 249	Carbohydrates: . . . . 34 g.
Total Fat:. . . . . 9 g.	Protein: . . . . 16 g.
Saturated Fat:. . . . . 1 g.	Cholesterol: . . . . 25 mg.
% Calories from Fat: 35	Sodium: . . . . 837 mg.

Turkey & Swiss Cheese Quiche

4 oz.	reduced fat Swiss cheese
4	white button mushrooms
1/4 small	white onion, peeled
1/4	green bell pepper, cored and seeded
1 cup	turkey, cooked and cut into 1/2-inch cubes
1 cup	nonfat milk
4	eggs, beaten (you may use egg substitute, if desired)
2 tbsp.	flour
1 tbsp.	instant chicken bouillon
1	9-inch unbaked pastry shell

Preheat the oven to 350°F. Attach the grating disc to the main body of the saladXPRESS™ and fasten it to the bowl, securing the safety latches. Use the slice/grate function and feed the cheese through the chute. Remove the cheese to a small bowl. Using the slicing disc slice the mushrooms, onion and the bell pepper. Remove the bowl and add to it the turkey, milk and eggs. Mix well.

In a separate bowl, mix together the cheese, flour and chicken bouillon and add it to the turkey mixture. Pour the quiche into the prepared pie shell. Bake for 40 to 45 minutes, until the center is firm to the touch. Let stand for 10 minutes before serving.

SERVES 4 TO 6.

Calories:. 313	Carbohydrates: . . . . 18 g.
Total Fat: . . . . 17 g.	Protein: . . . . 23 g.
Saturated Fat:. . . . . 5 g.	Cholesterol:. . . . . 186 mg.
% Calories from Fat: 32	Sodium: . . . . 489 mg.

Turkey Tacos with Chile Verde Salsa & Pistachios

1/2 lb.	boneless, skinless turkey breast, cooked
1	red onion, peeled and quartered
2 large	tomatoes, seeded
1	green bell pepper, seeded
4 oz.	reduced fat cheddar cheese
1/4 cup	unsalted pistachio nuts
8 small	lowfat flour tortillas, warmed
1 head	red leaf lettuce, washed, spin-dried and torn
1 cup	Chile Verde Salsa (see p. 30)

Attach the slicing disc to the main body of the saladXPRESS™ and fasten it to the bowl, securing the safety latches. Use the slice/grate function and feed the turkey through the chute. Remove the turkey and set aside. Using the slicing disc, slice the onion, tomatoes and bell pepper. Transfer each of the sliced vegetables individually to a single plate. Attach the grating disc and grate the cheddar cheese. Set aside. Grate the pistachios and set aside.

To serve, arrange 2 flour tortillas on each of 4 plates. Top each tortilla with the lettuce, turkey, onion, tomatoes and bell peppers. Place 1 table-spoon of Chile Verde Salsa over each taco and scatter with grated cheese. Garnish with the pistachio nuts. Serve the remaining salsa on the side.

❧ SERVES 4.

Calories:. 387		Carbohydrates: . . . . 44 g.	
Total Fat: . . . . 16 g.		Protein: . . . . 27 g.	
Saturated Fat:. . . . . 2 g.		Cholesterol: . . . . 51 mg.	
% Calories from Fat: 34		Sodium: . . . . 897 mg.	

Tropical Chicken & Papaya Salad

3	boneless, skinless chicken breast halves, cooked
1/4 small	pineapple, peeled and cut into sections
1/2	fresh papaya, peeled
1 small	red bell pepper, seeded
2 tbsp.	fresh parsley
2	green onions
1/2 cup	pineapple juice
2 tbsp.	sesame oil
2 tbsp.	rice vinegar
1/2 tsp.	salt
1/4 tsp.	black pepper
8 cups	mixed baby greens
1/4 cup	almonds, slivered

Attach the slicing disc to the main body of the saladXPRESS™ and fasten it to the bowl, securing the safety latches. Use the slice/grate function and feed the chicken through the chute. Repeat the process with the pineapple, papaya, bell pepper, parsley and onions. Toss to blend well.

In a separate bowl, combine the pineapple juice, sesame oil, vinegar, salt and pepper. Whisk vigorously until well blended. Drizzle the dressing over the chicken and toss. To serve, arrange the greens on four separate plates and top with the chicken salad. Sprinkle the almonds over the top of each to garnish.

✎ SERVES 4.

Calories:. 243	Carbohydrates: . . . . 22 g.
Total Fat: . . . . 11 g.	Protein: . . . . 16 g.
Saturated Fat:. . . . . <1 g.	Cholesterol: . . . . 31 mg.
% Calories from Fat: 40	Sodium: . . . . 373 mg.

Beef Ribeye Salad with Lemon Poppy Seed Dressing

1 1/2 lb.	beef ribeye steak, broiled, visible fat removed
3 small	Roma tomatoes, seeded
1 small	red onion, peeled and quartered
1 cup	fresh green beans, steamed tender-crisp
1 head	bibb lettuce, torn into bite sized pieces
1 head	red lettuce, torn into bite sized pieces
1 cup	canned or fresh mandarin oranges, sliced
1 cup	feta cheese, crumbled

Lemon Poppy Seed Dressing:

2 tbsp.	vegetable oil
1/4 cup	rice vinegar
2 tbsp.	water
2 tbsp.	chives, chopped
2 tbsp.	lemon juice
2 tbsp.	poppy seeds
1 tsp.	salt
1/2 tsp.	black pepper

Attach the slicing disc to the main body of the saladXPRESS™ and fasten it to the bowl, securing the safety latches. Use the slice/grate function and feed the beef through the chute. Repeat the process with the tomatoes and onions. Remove the bowl and add into it the green beans, both lettuces and the oranges. Toss gently to blend.

In a separate bowl, combine the oil, vinegar, water, chives, juice, poppy seeds, salt and pepper. Whisk well. Pour the dressing over the salad and toss gently. Top with the feta cheese.

 MAKES 6 SERVINGS.

Calories:. 365	Carbohydrates: . . . . 15 g.
Total Fat: . . . . 18 g.	Protein: . . . . 35 g.
Saturated Fat:. . . . . 8 g.	Cholesterol: . . . . 93 mg.
% Calories from Fat: 45	Sodium: . . . . 771 mg.

Thai Pork Salad

2 ribs	celery
1	green onion
1 large	radish
1/2 cup	canned water chestnuts, drained
1/2 lb.	boneless lean pork loin, cooked
1 cup	cooked brown rice
1 large	egg, scrambled (you may use egg substitute, if desired)
2 tbsp.	low sodium soy sauce
3 tsp.	rice vinegar
2 tsp.	peanut oil
1 clove	garlic, minced
1/2 tsp.	honey
1/4 tsp.	dry mustard
1/4 tsp.	ground ginger
8 large	romaine lettuce leaves

Attach the slicing disc to the main body of the saladXPRESS™ and fasten it to the bowl, securing the safety latches. Use the slice/grate function and feed the celery through the chute. Repeat the process with the onions, radish, water chestnuts and pork. Remove the bowl and add in the rice and egg. Toss lightly.

In a separate bowl, whisk together the soy sauce, vinegar, oil, garlic, honey, mustard and ginger. Pour the dressing over the Thai salad and toss again to blend. Serve on plates lined with lettuce leaves.

Calories:. 189	Carbohydrates: . . . . 17 g.
Total Fat:. . . . . 7 g.	Protein: . . . . 11 g.
Saturated Fat:. . . . . 4 g.	Cholesterol:. . . . . 106 mg.
% Calories from Fat: 57	Sodium: . . . . 324 mg.

Entrées &
Main Dish Salads

Hungarian Goulash

1/4 cup	all-purpose flour
1/2 tsp.	black pepper
1/2 tsp.	salt
1 lb.	lean beef, visible fat removed, cut into 1-inch cubes
1 tbsp.	vegetable oil
1 large	yellow onion, peeled
2 cloves	garlic
1 large	red bell pepper, seeded
8 small	new red potatoes, scrubbed and cut in half
2 1/2 cups	nonfat beef broth
3 tbsp.	all-purpose flour
2/3 cup	hot water
1 tbsp.	tomato sauce
1/2 cup	red vinegar
2 tsp.	sweet Hungarian paprika

Mix the flour, pepper and salt in a small plastic bag. Add the beef, a few pieces at a time, until all of the beef is covered with the flour. Heat the oil in a large stockpot on medium-high heat and sear the beef in batches on all sides, about 5 to 6 minutes total. Reduce the heat to medium.

Attach the slicing disc to the main body of the saladXPRESS™ and fasten it to the bowl, securing the safety latches. Use the slice/grate function and feed the onion, garlic, red pepper and potatoes through the chute. Add the vegetables to the beef and mix. Add the beef broth and heat to boiling. Mix together the flour and hot water until smooth and add to the broth. Stir and heat on medium until the stew is thickened. Add the tomato sauce, vinegar and paprika and reduce the heat to low. Heat and stir occasionally until the potatoes are tender and the beef is cooked through, about 1 hour.

❧ SERVES 4 TO 5.

Calories: *334*	*Carbohydrates:* . . . . *29 g.*
Total Fat: . . . . *10 g.*	*Protein:* . . . . *29 g.*
Saturated Fat: . . . . *3 g.*	*Cholesterol:* . . . . *54 mg.*
% Calories from Fat: *27*	*Sodium:* . . . . *378 mg.*

Tri-Tip Spinach Salad with Onion Herb Vinaigrette

3	tangelos, peeled and sectioned
2 cups	strawberries, washed and hulled
1 lb.	spinach, washed and spin-dried, torn
2 tbsp.	balsamic vinegar
2 tbsp.	extra virgin olive oil
1 tbsp.	lemon juice
1 tbsp.	fresh chives, minced
1 tbsp.	fresh parsley, minced
2 tsp.	Dijon mustard
1 tsp.	sugar
1/4 tsp.	ground thyme
1/4 tsp.	ground oregano
1/2 tsp.	salt
1/2 tsp.	black pepper
1 lb.	lean tri-tip steak, cooked and thinly sliced

Attach the slicing disc to the main body of the saladXPRESS™ and fasten it to the bowl, securing the safety latches. Use the slice/grate function and feed the tangelos through the chute. Repeat the process with the strawberries. Remove the bowl and add the spinach. Toss lightly.

In a separate bowl, combine the vinegar, oil, lemon juice, chives, parsley, mustard, sugar, thyme, oregano, salt and pepper. Whisk together well. Pour the dressing over the salad and toss again to coat. To serve, arrange the beef slices over the top of the salad.

❧ SERVES 4.

Calories: *388*	*Carbohydrates:* . . . . *20 g.*
Total Fat: . . . . *17 g.*	*Protein:* . . . . *38 g.*
Saturated Fat: . . . . *5 g.*	*Cholesterol:* . . . . *98 mg.*
% Calories from Fat: *40*	*Sodium:* . . . . *471 mg.*

Spicy-Orange Chicken Salad with Avocados

4	grilled, boneless, skinless chicken breast halves
1 small	tomato, seeded
1/2 small	red onion, peeled and quartered
1	ripe avocado, pitted
1/2 cup	sugar
1/4 cup	water
1/2 cup	red vinegar
1 cup	orange juice
1 tsp.	orange zest
1 tsp.	wasabi paste
1 tbsp.	lime juice
1 tbsp.	spicy salsa
8 cups	mixed salad greens, washed and spin-dried

Attach the slicing disc to the main body of the saladXPRESS™ and fasten it to the bowl, securing the safety latches. Use the slice/grate function and feed the chicken through the chute. Remove the bowl and set the chicken aside. Repeat the process with the tomato, onion and avocado.

In a large pan, heat the sugar and the water together over medium-high heat, stirring occasionally, until caramelized to a deep amber color. Remove from the heat and slowly add the vinegar. Return to the heat and stir until the sugar is completely dissolved. Stirring constantly, add the orange juice, zest and wasabi to taste. Place the chicken on a baking sheet and brush with the glaze. Bake at 350°F for

5 minutes until just heated through. Combine the lime juice, tomato, red onion, avocado and salsa. Spoon the vegetables over the salad greens and top with the warmed chicken.

SERVES 4 TO 6.

Calories:. 224	Carbohydrates: . . . . 29 g.
Total Fat:. . . . . 6 g.	Protein: . . . . 13 g.
Saturated Fat:. . . . . <1 g.	Cholesterol: . . . . 27 mg.
% Calories from Fat: 22	Sodium:. . . . . 74 mg.

Shredded Chicken Taco Salad

2	boneless, skinless chicken breasts, cooked
1 small	yellow onion, peeled and quartered
1 small	head iceberg lettuce, washed and spin-dried
1/2	head green cabbage, washed and cored
1 cup	reduced fat cheddar cheese
2 small	tomatoes
1 tsp.	salt
1/2 tsp.	chili powder
1/4 tsp.	black pepper
1/4 tsp.	ground cumin
1/4 tsp.	ground oregano
1/8 tsp.	red pepper flakes
2 cups	canned red kidney beans, rinsed and drained
2 cups	Colorful Garden Salsa (see p. 32)
10 oz.	pkg. baked tortilla chips
1/3 cup	lowfat sour cream

Attach the grating disc to the main body of the saladXPRESS™ and fasten it to the bowl, securing the safety latches. Use the slice/grate function and feed the chicken through the chute. Remove the chicken from the bowl and set aside. Grate the onion, lettuce, cabbage, cheddar cheese and tomatoes separately and place each in a separate bowl.

In a small container, combine the salt, chili powder, pepper, cumin, oregano and red pepper flakes. Add to the shredded chicken and mix thoroughly. Combine the beans, onions and salsa in a medium bowl and toss gently. Refrigerate both the chicken and the bean mixture until ready to serve. To serve, layer the tortilla chips in individual bowls. Top with the seasoned chicken and the bean mixture. Provide the grated lettuce, cabbage, cheese and tomatoes as accompaniments. Top with a small spoonful of the sour cream.

❧ SERVES 6 TO 8.

Calories:. 293	Carbohydrates: . . . . 50 g.
Total Fat:. . . . . 4 g.	Protein: . . . . 27 g.
Saturated Fat:. . . . . 1 g.	Cholesterol: . . . . 20 mg.
% Calories from Fat: 15	Sodium: . . . . 838 mg.

BBQ Smoked Chicken Pizza

1 large	purple onion, peeled and quartered
8 oz.	reduced fat mozzarella cheese
1/2 lb.	deli-style smoked boneless chicken
1	12-inch prepared pizza shell
1 cup	prepared barbecue sauce
2 tbsp.	fresh parsley, finely minced
2 tsp.	red pepper flakes

Attach the grating disc to the main body of the saladXPRESS™ and fasten it to the bowl, securing the safety latches. Use the slice/grate function and feed the onion through the chute. Set the onion aside. Grate the cheese and set aside. Attach the slicing disc to the main body of the saladXPRESS™ and slice the chicken.

Place the pizza shell on a baking sheet that has been sprinkled with cornmeal. Heat the oven to 400°F. Spread the barbecue sauce over the pizza shell and layer the chicken over the sauce. Scatter the onions over the chicken and sprinkle with parsley and red pepper flakes. Spread the cheese over the entire pizza. Bake for 12 to 15 minutes, until the cheese is melted and the pizza is bubbly.

❧ SERVES 6 TO 8.

Calories:	274	Carbohydrates:	46 g.
Total Fat:	7 g.	Protein:	17 g.
Saturated Fat:	<1 g.	Cholesterol:	29 mg.
% Calories from Fat:	18	Sodium:	932 mg.

Curry Chicken & Red Potato Salad

2 small	red onions, peeled and quartered
2 14 oz.	jars artichoke hearts, drained
6	boneless, skinless chicken breast halves, cooked
16 small	red potatoes, boiled
1/2 cup	nonfat plain yogurt
1/2 cup	lowfat mayonnaise
1 tbsp.	curry powder
1 head	butter lettuce, washed and spin-dried
	salt and pepper to taste

Attach the slicing disc to the main body of the saladXPRESS™ and fasten it to the bowl, securing the safety latches. Use the slice/grate function and feed the onions through the chute. Repeat the process with the artichoke hearts, chicken and potatoes. Toss the salad together and set aside.

In a separate bowl, combine the yogurt, mayonnaise and curry powder. Mix well and add to the chicken and potato salad. Toss again. Refrigerate for at least 2 hours, or until chilled. To serve, arrange the salad over the lettuce leaves and season the salad with salt and pepper.

☙ SERVES 12.

Calories:. 152	Carbohydrates: . . . . 22 g.
Total Fat:. . . . . 1 g.	Protein: . . . . 15 g.
Saturated Fat:. . . . . <1 g.	Cholesterol: . . . . 21 mg.
% Calories from Fat: 7	Sodium: . . . . 346 mg.

Sirloin Steak & Mushroom Salad

1 lb.	boneless beef sirloin steak, grilled and visible fat removed
1	red bell pepper, seeded
3	crimini mushrooms, scrubbed
1	sweet onion, peeled and quartered
3 cups	mixed baby salad greens, washed and spin-dried

Fresh Herb Dressing:

1	green onion
1 tbsp.	fresh parsley
1 tbsp.	fresh chives
2 tsp.	fresh tarragon
1 cup	lowfat mayonnaise
2 tbsp.	nonfat milk
1 tsp.	lemon juice

Attach the slicing disc to the main body of the saladXPRESS™ and fasten it to the bowl, securing the safety latches. Use the slice/grate function and feed the steak through the chute. Repeat the process with the bell pepper, mushrooms and onion. Transfer the steak and vegetables to another bowl and toss with the greens.

Attach the grating disc to the main body of the saladXPRESS™. Grate the green onion, parsley, chives and tarragon. Whisk together in a small bowl, the mayonnaise, milk and lemon juice. Add the herbs and onion and pour the dressing over the salad. Toss the salad again.

❧ SERVES 6.

Calories: *219*	*Carbohydrates:* . . . . *17 g.*
Total Fat: . . . . *8 g.*	*Protein:* . . . . *21 g.*
Saturated Fat: . . . . *2 g.*	*Cholesterol:* . . . . *47 mg.*
% Calories from Fat: *31*	*Sodium:* . . . . *437 mg.*

Honey-Mustard Chicken Salad

1 lb.	boneless, skinless chicken breasts, cooked
1/2 small	red onion, peeled and cut in half
2 ribs	celery
1/2 cup	golden raisins
1 tbsp.	lemon peel
1/2 cup	nonfat sour cream
1/4 cup	lowfat mayonnaise
2 tbsp.	lemon juice
2 tsp.	Dijon mustard
2 tsp.	honey
1 tbsp.	fresh rosemary, chopped
1/4 tsp.	salt
1/4 tsp.	black pepper
2 tsp.	lemon juice
1 tsp.	extra virgin olive oil
6	romaine lettuce leaves, washed and spin-dried
6	radicchio lettuce leaves, washed and spin-dried
1/4 cup	pine nuts, toasted
1 cup	garlic and cheese-flavored salad croutons

Attach the grating disc to the main body of the saladXPRESS™ and fasten it to the bowl, securing the safety latches. Use the slice/grate function and feed the chicken through the chute. Repeat the process with the onion. Reserve 2 tablespoons of grated onion. Attach the slicing disc to slice the celery. Remove the bowl and add in the raisins and lemon peel. Mix well and set aside.

In a separate bowl, combine the sour cream, mayonnaise, lemon juice, mustard, honey, rosemary, salt and pepper. Whisk well to blend. Toss the lemon juice and olive oil with the lettuce. To serve, divide the lettuce between 6 plates and top with the chicken and vegetables. Garnish with the reserved onion, a sprinkle of pine nuts and croutons. Serve with the dressing on the side.

~& MAKES 6 SERVINGS.

Calories: 259	*Carbohydrates:* . . . . 26 g.
Total Fat: . . . . 7 g.	*Protein:* . . . . 24 g.
Saturated Fat: . . . . <1 g.	*Cholesterol:* . . . . 47 mg.
% Calories from Fat: 24	*Sodium:* . . . . 359 mg.

Asian Crab & Cool Mint Salad

2	green onions
1 small	cucumber, peeled
1	carrot, peeled
1 cup	bean sprouts
1 clove	garlic
1	red chili
2 tsp.	fresh ginger
1/2 cup	fresh mint leaves, washed and spin-dried
1 tbsp.	fresh basil, washed and spin-dried
8 oz.	rice vermicelli, cooked
1/2 lb.	fresh crab meat, picked through and cooked

Sesame & Soy Dressing:

2 tbsp.	Oriental fish sauce
2 tbsp.	lime juice
1 tbsp.	sesame oil
2 tbsp.	low-sodium soy sauce
1 tbsp.	rice vinegar
2 tsp.	brown sugar
1 clove	garlic, minced

Attach the slicing disc to the main body of the saladXPRESS™ and fasten it to the bowl, securing the safety latches. Use the slice/grate function and feed the green onions, cucumber, carrot and bean sprouts through the chute. Remove the bowl and attach the grating disc. Grate the garlic, red chili, ginger, mint leaves and basil. Remove the main body, add the crab meat, and toss together well. Set aside.

In a separate bowl, whisk together the fish sauce, lime juice, sesame oil, soy sauce, vinegar, brown sugar and garlic. To serve, place the rice vermicelli on individual plates and top with the salad. Accompany with the dressing on the side.

❧ SERVES 4.

Calories:. 166	Carbohydrates: . . . . 21 g.
Total Fat:. . . . . 4 g.	Protein: . . . . 12 g.
Saturated Fat:. . . . . <1 g.	Cholesterol: . . . . 0 mg.
% Calories from Fat: 21	Sodium:. . . . . 997 mg.

Ginger Chicken Pasta Salad

2	boneless, skinless chicken breasts, cooked
6 to 8	green onions
3 medium	carrots, peeled
1 cup	unsalted peanuts, shelled
1 large	cucumber, peeled
1/4 cup	cilantro, washed and spin-dried
2 tsp.	fresh ginger, peeled and grated
3 cloves	garlic
1/4 cup	water
1/2 cup	low-sodium soy sauce
1/2 cup	rice vinegar
2 tbsp.	sugar
1/4 cup	sesame oil
2 tbsp.	Asian chile paste
2 lbs.	angel hair pasta, cooked al dente

Attach the slicing disc to the main body of the saladXPRESS™ and fasten it to the bowl, securing the safety latches. Use the slice/grate function and feed the chicken through the chute. Remove the bowl, transfer the chicken to a separate bowl and refrigerate.

Attach the grating disc and fasten the main body to the bowl. Feed the onions, carrots, peanuts, cucumber, cilantro, ginger and garlic through the chute to grate. Whisk together the water, soy sauce, vinegar, sugar, oil and chile paste and pour over the freshly grated vegetables. Add the chicken and pasta and toss well to blend.

✺ SERVES 12.

Calories:. 290	Carbohydrates: . . . . 34 g.
Total Fat:. . . . . 11 g.	Protein: . . . . 14 g.
Saturated Fat:. . . . . 1 g.	Cholesterol: . . . . 7 mg.
% Calories from Fat: 35	Sodium: . . . . 409 mg.

Pepper Jack Turkey Salad

1 lb.	boneless, skinless turkey breast, cooked
10	whole ripe olives, pitted
1	cucumber, peeled
1/2 bunch	fresh cilantro, washed and spin-dried
8 oz.	reduced fat Pepper Jack cheese
2 cups	ziti pasta, cooked al dente

Salsa Dressing:

3/4 cup	nonfat plain yogurt
2 tbsp.	lowfat mayonnaise
2 tbsp.	nonfat milk
1/2 cup	Colorful Garden Salsa (see p. 32)

Attach the slicing disc to the main body of the saladXPRESS™ and fasten it to the bowl, securing the safety latches. Use the slice/grate function and feed the turkey through the chute. Repeat the process with the olives and cucumber. Set aside and attach the grating disc to the saladXPRESS™. Grate the cilantro and cheese. Toss the cilantro and cheese with the turkey, olives and cucumber.

In a medium bowl, mix together the yogurt, mayonnaise, milk and salsa. Add the cooked pasta to the dressing and toss to coat. Add the pasta and dressing to the remaining ingredients and toss again. Cover and chill for 1 hour before serving.

❧ SERVES 4.

Calories:. 290	Carbohydrates: . . . . 21 g.
Total Fat: . . . . 12 g.	Protein: . . . . 21 g.
Saturated Fat:. . . . . 4 g.	Cholesterol: . . . . 47 mg.
% Calories from Fat: 31	Sodium: . . . . 430 mg.

Fresh Asparagus & Ham Salad

1/2 lb.	ham, cooked
1	pineapple, peeled, cored and cut into large pieces
1 cup	fresh asparagus tips, blanched
1/2 cup	nonfat plain yogurt
1/2 cup	lowfat mayonnaise
1	chive, finely minced
1/4 tsp.	salt
1/4 tsp.	black pepper
8 cups	mixed salad greens, washed and spin-dried
1/2 cup	crispy chow mein noodles

Attach the slicing disc to the main body of the saladXPRESS™ and fasten it to the bowl, securing the safety latches. Use the slice/grate function and feed the ham through the chute. Repeat the process to slice the pineapple and asparagus. Remove the bowl and mix well.

In a separate bowl, combine the yogurt, mayonnaise, chive, salt and pepper. Blend well.

To serve, arrange the ham, pineapple and asparagus over the salad greens on 8 individual plates. Drizzle each salad with dressing and garnish with crispy noodles.

❧ SERVES 8.

Calories:. 128		Carbohydrates: . . . . 18 g.	
Total Fat:. . . . . 4 g.		Protein:. . . . . 7 g.	
Saturated Fat:. . . . . <1 g.		Cholesterol: . . . . 21 mg.	
% Calories from Fat: 26		Sodium:. . . . . 598 mg.	

Chicken, Black Bean & Avocado Salad

2	boneless, skinless chicken breasts, cooked
1/2 head	green cabbage, washed and cored
8	plum tomatoes
4	green onions
1/2 small	purple onion
1	red bell pepper, seeded
1 1/2 cups	frozen corn, thawed
15 oz.	can black beans, rinsed and drained
1/2 head	romaine lettuce, washed, spin-dried and torn
2	avocados, peeled, pitted and sliced
6 oz.	reduced fat Monterey Jack cheese
1 cup	Sun-Dried Tomato & Chile Salsa (see p. 28)

Garlic Dressing:

1 tbsp.	vegetable oil
1/4 cup	cider vinegar
3 tbsp.	honey
1 1/2 tsp.	ground cumin
1 tbsp.	lemon juice
1 clove	garlic, minced
1/4 tsp.	salt
1/4 tsp.	black pepper

Attach the slicing disc to the main body of the saladXPRESS™ and fasten it to the bowl, securing the safety latches. Use the slice/grate function and feed the chicken through the chute. Set the chicken aside. Repeat the process to slice the cabbage, tomato, onions and the red pepper. Add the chicken, corn, beans and torn romaine leaves to the sliced vegetables and mix well.

In a small bowl, whisk together the oil, vinegar, honey, cumin, lemon juice, garlic, salt and pepper. Pour the dressing over the salad and toss to coat. Using the slicing disc, slice the avocados and set aside. Attach the grating disc to the saladXPRESS™ and grate the cheese. Pass the salsa, cheese and avocados at the table.

❧ SERVES 4 TO 6.

Calories:. 372	Carbohydrates: . . . . 49 g.
Total Fat: . . . . 16 g.	Protein: . . . . 17 g.
Saturated Fat:. . . . . 2 g.	Cholesterol: . . . . 39 mg.
% Calories from Fat: 42	Sodium: . . . . 694 mg.

Grilled Chicken Salad with Honey Soy Dressing

2	boneless, skinless chicken breasts, grilled
1	bell pepper, seeded
1 large	carrot, peeled
8	green onions
1/2 lb.	sugar snap peas, cut in half
1/2 lb.	fusilli pasta, cooked al dente
1 tbsp.	sesame seeds, toasted

Honey Soy Dressing:

1/4 cup	rice vinegar
2 tbsp.	honey
1 tbsp.	vegetable oil
2 tsp.	sesame oil
1 tbsp.	low sodium soy sauce

Attach the slicing disc to the main body of the saladXPRESS™ and fasten it to the bowl, securing the safety latches. Use the slice/grate function and feed the chicken through the chute. Repeat the process with the pepper, carrot and onions. Remove the bowl and add in the sugar snap peas and pasta. Mix well.

In a separate bowl, whisk together the vinegar, honey, oil, sesame oil and soy sauce. Pour the dressing over the salad and toss lightly. Sprinkle the sesame seeds over the salad and serve immediately.

❧ SERVES 4.

Calories:. 293		Carbohydrates: . . . . 39 g.	
Total Fat:. . . . . 6 g.		Protein: . . . . 16 g.	
Saturated Fat:. . . . . <1 g.		Cholesterol: . . . . 21 mg.	
% Calories from Fat: 21		Sodium: . . . . 165 mg.	

Turkey & Asparagus Salad with Summer Berries

3 stalks	fresh asparagus, steamed until tender-crisp
1 cup	fresh green beans, trimmed
1	boneless, skinless turkey breast, cooked
2 cups	strawberries, washed
10 cups	baby spinach, washed and spin-dried
1/2 cup	fresh raspberries, washed

Raspberry Dressing:

1 cup	nonfat vanilla yogurt
2 tbsp.	mint leaves, finely chopped
1/4 cup	nonfat mayonnaise
2 tbsp.	honey
1/4 cup	raspberry vinegar

Attach the slicing disc to the main body of the saladXPRESS™ and fasten it to the bowl, securing the safety latches. Use the slice/grate function and feed the asparagus through the chute. Repeat the process with the green beans, turkey breast and strawberries. Remove the bowl and toss in the spinach and raspberries.

In a separate bowl, whisk together the yogurt, mint, mayonnaise, honey and vinegar. Pour the dressing over the salad and toss.

SERVES 4.

Calories: 196	Carbohydrates: . . . . 30 g.
Total Fat: . . . . 3 g.	Protein: . . . . 14 g.
Saturated Fat: . . . . <1 g.	Cholesterol: . . . . 22 mg.
% Calories from Fat: 12	Sodium: . . . . 241 mg.

Santa Barbara Chicken Salad

1	boneless, skinless chicken breast, cooked
1	medium tomato, seeded
1 small	green bell pepper, seeded
1 small	red bell pepper, seeded
1 small	purple onion, peeled and quartered
2 cups	frozen peas, thawed and drained
1/2 tsp.	salt
1/2 tsp.	black pepper
1/2 cup	nonfat mayonnaise
1/2 tsp.	sugar
10	roasted almonds, chopped

Attach the slicing disc to the main body of the saladXPRESS™ and fasten it to the bowl, securing the safety latches. Use the slice/grate function and feed the chicken through the chute. Repeat the process with the tomato, green pepper, red pepper and onion. Remove the bowl and add in the peas. Sprinkle with the salt and pepper. Smooth the mayonnaise completely over the top of the salad and sprinkle with the sugar. Cover tightly with plastic wrap and refrigerate for 8 hours or overnight. Just before serving, sprinkle the almonds over the top of the salad.

SERVES 4.

Calories:. 139	Carbohydrates: . . . . 20 g.
Total Fat:. . . . . 2 g.	Protein:. . . . . 9 g.
Saturated Fat:. . . . . <1 g.	Cholesterol: . . . . 10 mg.
% Calories from Fat: 15	Sodium:. . . . . 625 mg.

Grilled Turkey & Apple Cole Slaw

2	boneless, skinless turkey breast halves, grilled
2	red apples, peeled and cored
1 rib	celery
3/4 cup	walnut halves
1/2 cup	lowfat sour cream
1/2 cup	nonfat plain yogurt
2 tbsp.	lemon juice
1/2 tsp.	black pepper

Attach the grating disc to the main body of the saladXPRESS™ and fasten it to the bowl, securing the safety latches. Use the slice/grate function and feed the turkey through the chute. Repeat the process with the apples, celery and walnuts. Remove the bowl and toss to blend.

In a separate bowl, combine the sour cream, yogurt, lemon juice, and pepper. Whisk together well and pour the dressing over the salad. Toss to coat. Chill or serve at once.

SERVES 4.

Calories:. 315	Carbohydrates: . . . . 26 g.
Total Fat: . . . . 17 g.	Protein: . . . . 20 g.
Saturated Fat:. . . . . 1 g.	Cholesterol: . . . . 31 mg.
% Calories from Fat: 45	Sodium: . . . . 523 mg.

Fire-Roasted Peppers & Smoked Turkey Salad

1/2 lb.	boneless, skinless smoked turkey breast
1 small	zucchini, ends removed
1 small	purple onion, peeled and quartered
1 small	green bell pepper, seeded
1 small	red bell pepper, seeded
10	cherry tomatoes, halved
1 lb.	farfelle pasta, cooked al dente and drained

Fire-Roasted Pepper Dressing:

6 oz.	fire-roasted peppers, drained
1/4	lemon with peel
2 tbsp.	lemon juice, fresh squeezed
3/4 cup	nonfat plain yogurt
1/2 tsp.	ground black pepper

Attach the slicing disc to the main body of the saladXPRESS™ and fasten it to the bowl, securing the safety latches. Use the slice/grate function and feed the turkey through the chute. Repeat the process with the zucchini, onion, green pepper and red pepper. Remove the bowl and add the cherry tomatoes and pasta to the vegetables and turkey.

Combine the fire-roasted peppers, lemon, lemon juice, yogurt and pepper in a blender and puree. Pour the dressing over the salad and blend well. Refrigerate for 1 hour before serving.

Calories:. 311	Carbohydrates: . . . . 53 g.
Total Fat:. . . . . 2 g.	Protein: . . . . 24 g.
Saturated Fat:. . . . . <1 g.	Cholesterol: . . . . 22 mg.
% Calories from Fat: 4	Sodium: . . . . 552 mg.

Entrées &
Main Dish Salads

Grilled Shrimp with Strawberry & Melon Slaw

1 cup	watermelon, grated
1 cup	cantaloupe, grated
1 cup	honeydew, grated
2 cups	strawberries, grated
1 cup	nonfat lemon yogurt
1 tsp.	lemon juice
1/2 tsp.	lemon zest
1 tbsp.	honey
1 lb.	medium shrimp, shelled, deveined and grilled

Attach the grating disc to the main body of the saladXPRESS™ and fasten it to the bowl, securing the safety latches. Use the slice/grate function and feed the watermelon through the chute. Repeat the process with the cantaloupe, honeydew and strawberries. Remove the bowl and toss gently. Refrigerate until ready to serve.

In a separate bowl, combine the yogurt, lemon juice, zest and honey. Whisk together well. Just before serving, pour the dressing over the salad. Toss gently to coat. Top each serving with the grilled shrimp.

∽ SERVES 4.

Calories:. 240	Carbohydrates: . . . . 28 g.
Total Fat:. . . . . 2 g.	Protein: . . . . 26 g.
Saturated Fat:. . . . . <1 g.	Cholesterol:. . . . . 172 mg.
% Calories from Fat: 9	Sodium: . . . . 213 mg.

Chile Chicken Cole Slaw

1/2 head	green cabbage, washed and cored
1/2 head	purple cabbage, washed and cored
2	boneless, skinless chicken breast halves, cooked
1	red apple, peeled and cored
1 cup	green grapes
1 cup	diced green chiles
1/2 cup	nonfat sour cream
1/2 cup	nonfat mayonnaise
1 tbsp.	honey
1 tbsp.	lime juice
	salt and pepper to taste
1/4 cup	walnut halves

Attach the grating disc to the main body of the saladXPRESS™ and fasten it to the bowl, securing the safety latches. Use the slice/grate function and feed the green and purple cabbage through the chute. Repeat the process with the chicken, apple and grapes. Remove the bowl and add the chiles. Toss the salad gently.

In a separate bowl, combine the sour cream, mayonnaise, honey and lime juice. Stir to blend well. Pour the dressing over the salad and toss to coat. Season with salt and pepper. Use the grating disc to grate the walnuts and set aside. Refrigerate the salad for at least 1 hour. Just before serving, top the salad with the walnuts.

SERVES 6.

Calories:. 220	Carbohydrates: . . . . 31 g.
Total Fat:. . . . . 6 g.	Protein: . . . . 12 g.
Saturated Fat:. . . . . 1 g.	Cholesterol: . . . . 22 mg.
% Calories from Fat: 25	Sodium: . . . . 372 mg.

Chinese Tofu Salad with Peanut Vinaigrette

8 oz.	firm tofu
1 small	head green cabbage, washed and cored
2	carrots, peeled
1 medium	cucumber, peeled
1/3 cup	fresh cilantro
6 oz.	Chinese wheat noodles, cooked, drained and rinsed
1 cup	fresh bean sprouts

Peanut Vinaigrette:

1/4 cup	lowfat peanut butter
1 tbsp.	low sodium soy sauce
1 tbsp.	rice vinegar
1 tsp.	dark sesame oil
1 clove	garlic, minced

In a small bowl, whisk together the peanut butter, soy sauce, vinegar, sesame oil and garlic. Set aside.

Attach the slicing disc to the main body of the saladXPRESS™ and fasten it to the bowl, securing the safety latches. Use the slice/grate function and feed the tofu through the chute. Repeat the process with the cabbage, carrots, cucumber and cilantro. Remove the bowl and add the noodles and sprouts. Mix together well. Pour the dressing over the salad and toss to coat. Chill before serving.

Calories:. 368	Carbohydrates: . . . . 58 g.
Total Fat:. . . . . 9 g.	Protein: . . . . 19 g.
Saturated Fat:. . . . . 1 g.	Cholesterol: . . . . 0 mg.
% Calories from Fat: 21	Sodium: . . . . 653 mg.

Chapter 3

Vegetables
& Side Dishes

Sautéed Green Beans with Feta Cheese & Walnuts

3/4 lb.	fresh green beans, washed and drained
1 tsp.	extra virgin olive oil
2 tbsp.	lowfat margarine
1/3 cup	walnut halves
1/2 cup	feta cheese, crumbled

Attach the slicing disc to the main body of the saladXPRESS™ and fasten it to the bowl, securing the safety latches. Use the slice/grate function and feed the green beans through the chute. Slice the green beans into bite-size pieces.

In a nonstick sauté pan over medium-high heat, cook the green beans in the olive oil until the beans are just crisp-tender. Spoon the beans into a serving bowl and keep warm. Attach the grating disc to the saladXPRESS™ and fasten it to the bowl. Grate the walnuts. Place the margarine in the sauté pan over medium heat and sauté the walnuts until they are lightly toasted. Add the walnuts to the warm green beans and toss together with the feta cheese. Serve immediately.

SERVES 4.

Calories:	153	Carbohydrates:	6 g.
Total Fat:	12 g.	Protein:	5 g.
Saturated Fat:	4 g.	Cholesterol:	17 mg.
% Calories from Fat:	71	Sodium:	275 mg.

Lemon & Tri-Pepper Sauté

1	red bell pepper, seeded
1	yellow bell pepper, seeded
1	green bell pepper, seeded
1 lb.	fresh broccoli, washed and cut in florets
2 tbsp.	lowfat margarine
1 tsp.	lemon peel, finely grated
1 tbsp.	lemon juice
1 tbsp.	fresh thyme, chopped

Attach the slicing disc to the main body of the saladXPRESS™ and fasten it to the bowl, securing the safety latches. Use the slice/grate function and feed the red pepper through the chute. Repeat the process with the remaining bell peppers. Place the peppers and the broccoli in a saucepan steamer basket over simmering water. Cover and steam for 8 to 12 minutes, or until the vegetables are just crisp-tender.

In a small saucepan over low heat, melt the margarine and add the lemon peel, lemon juice and the fresh thyme. Stir to combine well. Place the steamed vegetables on a serving platter and drizzle the lemon sauce over all.

❧ SERVES 6.

Calories: 53	Carbohydrates: . . . . 10 g.
Total Fat: . . . . 1 g.	Protein: . . . . 3 g.
Saturated Fat: . . . . <1 g.	Cholesterol: . . . . 0 mg.
% Calories from Fat: 20	Sodium: . . . . 59 mg.

Sweet Honey-Spiced Carrots

1 lb.	carrots, peeled
1 tbsp.	lowfat margarine
2 tbsp.	honey
1/8 tsp.	ground ginger
1/8 tsp.	ground cinnamon
dash	ground cloves

Attach the slicing disc to the main body of the saladXPRESS™ and fasten it to the bowl, securing the safety latches. Use the slice/grate function and feed the carrots through the chute. Cut the carrots into 1/4-inch slices. Place the sliced carrots into a saucepan steamer basket over simmering water. Cover and simmer for 5 to 7 minutes until the carrots are crisp-tender. Place the carrots in a serving bowl and keep warm.

In a small saucepan over low heat, melt the margarine and honey together, stirring to blend well. Add the ginger, cinnamon and cloves and whisk. Pour the sauce over the carrots and toss to coat. Serve immediately.

❧ SERVES 4.

Calories: 86	Carbohydrates: . . . . 20 g.
Total Fat: . . . . <1 g.	Protein: . . . . 1 g.
Saturated Fat: . . . . <1 g.	Cholesterol: . . . . 0 mg.
% Calories from Fat: 10	Sodium: . . . . 67 mg.

Summer Vegetable Bake

1 1/2 lbs.	yellow summer squash
2	red onions, peeled and quartered
8	plum tomatoes
2 tbsp.	lowfat margarine
1 tbsp.	fresh basil, minced
1/4 cup	Parmesan cheese, grated
1 1/2 cups	herbed bread croutons
	salt and pepper to taste

Preheat the oven to 350°F. Attach the slicing disc to the main body of the saladXPRESS™ and fasten it to the bowl, securing the safety latches. Use the slice/grate function and feed the squash through the chute. Slice into 1/8-inch slices. Repeat the process with the onions and tomatoes.

Layer half of the vegetables in a 9" x 13" baking pan. Dot 1 tablespoon of the margarine over the vegetables. Sprinkle the basil, salt and pepper and half of the Parmesan cheese over the margarine. Layer the remaining vegetables and sprinkle the remaining Parmesan cheese over the top. Attach the grating disc to the saladXPRESS™ and feed the croutons through the chute. Layer the crushed croutons on top of the cheese and dot with the remaining margarine. Bake for 45 to 60 minutes, until the squash is tender.

SERVES 6.

Calories:	133	Carbohydrates:	19 g.
Total Fat:	5 g.	Protein:	5 g.
Saturated Fat:	2 g.	Cholesterol:	3 mg.
% Calories from Fat:	31	Sodium:	272 mg.

Fresh Vegetable Ratatouille

2 small	zucchini, ends removed
6	firm Roma tomatoes
1 small	eggplant, peeled and sliced lengthwise into quarters
2 ribs	celery
1	green bell pepper, quartered
1 clove	garlic, minced
1 small	onion, quartered
1 tbsp.	extra virgin olive oil
1/4 cup	chili sauce
2 tsp.	sugar
1 tbsp.	fresh parsley, minced
1/4 tsp.	black pepper
1/2 tsp.	dried oregano
1/2 tsp.	dried basil

Attach the slicing disc to the main body of the saladXPRESS™ and fasten it to the bowl, securing the safety latches. Use the slice/grate function and feed the zucchini through the chute. Slice the zucchini into 1/4-inch slices. Repeat the process with the remaining vegetables, slicing the onion last.

In a large skillet over medium heat, sauté the garlic and onion in the olive oil until the onion is translucent. Add the remaining vegetables to the skillet and toss together. Add the chili sauce, sugar, parsley, pepper, oregano and basil and stir to combine. Reduce the heat

to low, cover and simmer for 30 to 45 minutes, or until the vegetables
are tender.

SERVES 5.

Calories: *118*	*Carbohydrates:* . . . . *22 g.*
Total Fat: . . . . *3 g.*	*Protein:* . . . . *3 g.*
Saturated Fat: . . . . *<1 g.*	*Cholesterol:* . . . . *0 mg.*
% Calories from Fat: *24*	*Sodium:* . . . . *419 mg.*

Vegetables &
Side Dishes

Hot Skillet Potatoes

4	new red potatoes, scrubbed and quartered
2	green onions
2 sprigs	fresh parsley
1 tsp.	extra virgin olive oil
1/4 tsp.	black pepper
2 cloves	garlic, minced
1 slice	turkey bacon, cooked and crumbled
1 tbsp.	lowfat margarine, melted

Attach the slicing disc to the main body of the saladXPRESS™ and fasten it to the bowl, securing the safety latches. Use the slice/grate function and feed the potatoes through the chute. Slice the potatoes into 1/4-inch slices. Repeat the process with the green onions and parsley.

Preheat the oven to 400°F. Using an ovenproof skillet, drizzle the olive oil in the skillet and swirl to coat the bottom and sides of the skillet. Layer half of the potatoes around the pan, beginning in the center and moving toward the edges of the pan. Sprinkle the potatoes with half of the pepper, then top with the green onions, garlic, bacon and the fresh parsley. Add the remaining potato slices and press down with a large spatula to compress the potatoes. Drizzle with the margarine and sprinkle the remaining pepper on top.

Cook the potatoes on medium-high heat on the stove, shaking the pan occasionally, until the potatoes are crisp and brown on the bottom. Remove the skillet from the burner and place it in the oven. Bake for 15 minutes until the potatoes are tender. Remove the skillet from the oven and carefully loosen the edges of the potatoes. Invert the potatoes onto a serving platter. To serve, cut into wedges.

MAKES 4 SERVINGS.

Calories: 74	*Carbohydrates:* . . . . 10 g.
Total Fat:. . . . . 3 g.	*Protein:*. . . . . 4 g.
Saturated Fat:. . . . . <1 g.	*Cholesterol:* . . . . 3 mg.
% Calories from Fat: 29	*Sodium:*. . . . . 89 mg.

Couscous & Mint-Stuffed Yellow Peppers

1 large	yellow onion, peeled and quartered
2 cloves	garlic
1 sprig	fresh thyme
1 sprig	fresh mint
1 bunch	fresh parsley
3	yellow bell peppers, cut in half and seeded
1 tsp.	extra virgin olive oil
1 tsp.	lemon juice
1 2/3 cups	fat free chicken broth
1 1/4 cups	couscous
	salt and pepper to taste
2 tbsp.	feta cheese, crumbled

Attach the grating disc to the main body of the saladXPRESS™ and fasten it to the bowl, securing the safety latches. Use the slice/grate function and feed the onion and garlic through the chute. Remove the vegetables and reattach the grating disc. Feed the thyme, mint and parsley through the chute.

Place the pepper halves, cut side down, in a 12" x 17" baking pan. Bake at 450°F for 10 to 15 minutes. Remove from the heat. Sauté the onion and garlic in the oil in a large sauté pan for 3 minutes, or until the vegetables are tender. Add the herbs and stir. Add the lemon juice, broth and couscous. Bring to a boil, then cover and remove from the heat. Let stand for 3 to 4 minutes until the couscous is tender.

Fill each pepper half with couscous and sprinkle the cheese over the peppers. Bake at 350°F for 5 minutes and serve.

❧ SERVES 6.

Calories: *93*	*Carbohydrates:* . . . . *17 g.*
Total Fat:. . . . . *2 g.*	*Protein:*. . . . . *4 g.*
Saturated Fat:. . . . . *<1 g.*	*Cholesterol:* . . . . *4 mg.*
% Calories from Fat: *16*	*Sodium:* . . . . *174 mg.*

Sautéed Red Cabbage with Bacon & Onions

8 slices	turkey bacon
2 large	yellow onions, quartered
1 large	head red cabbage, halved and cored
3 tbsp.	lowfat margarine
1 tbsp.	sugar
2 tbsp.	red vinegar
1 3/4 cups	fat-free chicken broth
1/2 cup	apple cider vinegar
1 tbsp.	cornstarch
1/2 tsp.	salt
1/4 tsp.	freshly ground black pepper

In a large skillet over medium-high heat, sauté the bacon until it is crisp. Crumble and set aside. Attach the slicing disc to the main body of the saladXPRESS™ and fasten it to the bowl, securing the safety latches. Use the slice/grate function and feed the onions through the chute. Attach the grating disc to the saladXPRESS™ and grate the cabbage.

Melt the margarine in the skillet. Add the onions and sauté for 3 minutes, or until they are translucent. Add the red cabbage and cook, stirring frequently, for 3 minutes. Add the crumbled bacon, sugar, vinegar, chicken broth and cider vinegar. Bring to a boil, reduce the heat to low and simmer, covered, for 30 minutes. The cabbage will be soft and tender when done. Mix the cornstarch with a small amount of water until smooth. Add to the sauce in the skillet and bring to a boil. Reduce the heat to low and season with the salt and pepper. Serve immediately.

~&~ MAKES 8 SERVINGS.

Calories:. 114		Carbohydrates: . . . . 16 g.	
Total Fat:. . . . . 4 g.		Protein:. . . . . 5 g.	
Saturated Fat:. . . . . 1 g.		Cholesterol: . . . . 10 mg.	
% Calories from Fat: 31		Sodium: . . . . 519 mg.	

Vegetables & Side Dishes

Tomato & Mozzarella Cheese Strata

1	baguette French bread
8	Roma tomatoes
4 oz.	reduced fat mozzarella cheese
1/4	red onion, peeled
2 cloves	garlic
3 tbsp.	lowfat margarine, divided
4	eggs (you may use egg substitute, if desired)
4 slices	turkey bacon, cooked and crumbled
2 tsp.	sugar
1 tbsp.	fresh oregano, minced
1 tsp.	fresh parsley, minced
1 tsp.	fresh basil, minced
1/2 tsp.	ground black pepper

Attach the slicing disc to the main body of the saladXPRESS™ and fasten it to the bowl, securing the safety latches. Use the slice/grate function and feed the bread through the chute. Repeat the process with the Roma tomatoes. Replace the slicing disc with the grating disc and grate the mozzarella cheese. Set aside. Grate the onion and garlic and set aside.

Preheat the oven to 400°F. Spread both sides of the bread slices with margarine and place the slices on a baking sheet. Bake for 3 minutes on each side of the bread, until lightly toasted. Reduce the heat to 350°F.

Coat a 7" x 11" baking pan with nonstick cooking spray. Sauté the onion and garlic in a large sauté pan in the remaining butter until the vegetables are tender. In a large bowl, lightly beat the eggs. Stir in the sautéed vegetables, bacon, sugar, oregano, parsley, basil and black pepper. Arrange the bread slices in the bottom of the baking pan. Pour the egg batter over the top of the bread. Arrange the tomato slices over the top of the casserole. Sprinkle with the cheese and bake, uncovered, for 30 to 35 minutes, or until a knife inserted near the center comes out clean. Serve immediately.

◣ MAKES 6 TO 8 SERVINGS.

Calories:. 290	Carbohydrates: . . . . 44 g.
Total Fat:. . . . . 8 g.	Protein: . . . . 15 g.
Saturated Fat:. . . . . 2 g.	Cholesterol:. . . . . 119 mg.
% Calories from Fat: 25	Sodium: . . . . 674 mg.

Cheddar & Dill
Yukon Gold Potatoes

4 oz.	reduced fat sharp cheddar cheese
6 medium	Yukon Gold potatoes, peeled and quartered
1 large	white onion, peeled and quartered
1/4 cup	all-purpose flour
1 tsp.	fresh dill weed, minced
1 tsp.	salt
1/4 tsp.	black pepper
2 cups	nonfat milk

Attach the grating disc to the main body of the saladXPRESS™ and fasten it to the bowl, securing the safety latches. Use the slice/grate function and feed the cheese through the chute. Remove the grated cheese from the bowl and set aside. Attach the slicing disc and feed the potatoes through the chute. Slice the potatoes into 1/4-inch slices. Repeat the process with the onion. Set aside.

Sift together the flour, dill, salt and pepper in a saucepan. Over medium heat, whisk the milk into the flour until no lumps remain. Heat and stir until the sauce thickens and boils. Reduce the heat to low and add the cheddar cheese, whisking until the cheese is melted. Remove the saucepan from the heat.

Preheat the oven to 375°F. Lightly spray a 2-quart baking dish with cooking spray. Place half of the potatoes and half of the onions in the pan. Top with half of the sauce. Repeat the layers, pouring the last of the sauce over the potatoes. Cover the casserole and bake for 1 1/2 hours, or until the potatoes are tender. Remove the cover and brown the potatoes during the last few minutes of cooking.

⋆ SERVES 6.

Calories:. 159	Carbohydrates: . . . . 21 g.
Total Fat:. . . . . 5 g.	Protein: . . . . 13 g.
Saturated Fat:. . . . . <1 g.	Cholesterol: . . . . 22 mg.
% Calories from Fat: 27	Sodium:. . . . . 438 mg.

Zesty Crisp Onions

3 large	yellow onions, peeled and quartered
	cold water
1 tsp.	all-purpose flour
1 tsp.	seasoned salt
1/4 tsp.	black pepper
1/4 tsp.	cayenne pepper
1/2 tsp.	paprika
1 tbsp.	vegetable oil

Attach the slicing disc to the main body of the saladXPRESS™ and fasten it to the bowl, securing the safety latches. Use the slice/grate function and feed the onions through the chute. Slice the onions 1/2-inch thick. Place the onion slices in a large bowl and pour the cold water over to cover. Refrigerate for 30 minutes. Drain the onions well in a colander.

Mix together in a medium bowl, the flour, salt, pepper, cayenne and the paprika. Preheat the oven to 375°F. Coat a large baking sheet with nonstick cooking spray. Place the onions on the baking sheet and spray with nonstick cooking spray. Sprinkle the seasonings over the onions. Bake for 10 to 15 minutes, or until the onions are crisp.

꙾ MAKES 4 SERVINGS.

Calories:	78	Carbohydrates:	11 g.
Total Fat:	4 g.	Protein:	2 g.
Saturated Fat:	<1 g.	Cholesterol:	0 mg.
% Calories from Fat:	40	Sodium:	329 mg.

Spiced Louisiana Sweet Potatoes

6 medium	yams, scrubbed and quartered
1 cup	nonfat milk
1 tsp.	ground nutmeg
1/2 tsp.	ground cardamom
2	eggs (you may use egg substitute, if desired)
1 cup	dark brown sugar, packed
1/4 cup	lowfat margarine, melted

Preheat the oven to 400°F. Attach the grating disc to the main body of the saladXPRESS™ and fasten it to the bowl, securing the safety latches. Use the slice/grate function and feed the yams through the chute. Add the milk, nutmeg, cardamom, eggs and the brown sugar to the bowl of potatoes and mix well. Spread the potatoes into a 9" x 13" baking pan that has been coated with nonstick cooking spray. Pour the melted margarine over the yams. Bake for 30 minutes, until the yams are soft.

SERVES 6.

Calories:. 278	Carbohydrates: . . . . 71 g.
Total Fat:. . . . . 5 g.	Protein:. . . . . 7 g.
Saturated Fat:. . . . . 1 g.	Cholesterol: . . . . 72 mg.
% Calories from Fat: 24	Sodium:. . . . . 93 mg.

Carrots & Water Chestnuts in Herbs

1 lb.	carrots, scraped
2 tbsp.	lowfat margarine
6 oz.	can water chestnuts, drained
2 tsp.	fresh thyme, minced
1 tbsp.	fresh parsley, minced
2 tsp.	fresh basil, minced
3 tbsp.	rice vinegar

Attach the slicing disc to the main body of the saladXPRESS™ and fasten it to the bowl, securing the safety latches. Use the slice/grate function and feed the carrots through the chute. Cut the carrots into 1/4-inch slices. Repeat the process with the water chestnuts. Place the carrots in a saucepan steamer basket over boiling water and steam for 6 minutes, or until just tender.

In a large sauté pan over medium-low heat, melt the margarine and add the water chestnuts, thyme, parsley and the basil and cook for 2 minutes. Add the steamed carrots and the vinegar and warm just until thoroughly heated. Serve immediately.

SERVES 5.

Calories: 73	Carbohydrates: . . . . 14 g.
Total Fat:. . . . . 2 g.	Protein:. . . . . 1 g.
Saturated Fat:. . . . . <1 g.	Cholesterol: . . . . 0 mg.
% Calories from Fat: 17	Sodium:. . . . . 81 mg.

Breakfast Ham & Cheese Quiche

3 large	baking potatoes, scrubbed and quartered
5	green onions
1 tbsp.	lowfat margarine
1 tsp.	black pepper
8 oz.	lean cooked ham
1	green bell pepper, seeded
2 oz.	reduced fat sharp cheddar cheese
10 3/4 oz.	can lowfat cream of chicken soup
2	eggs, beaten (use egg substitute, if desired)

Vegetables &
Side Dishes

Attach the grating disc to the main body of the saladXPRESS™ and fasten it to the bowl, securing the safety latches. Use the slice/grate function and feed the potatoes through the chute. Repeat the process with the green onions. Remove the bowl and add the margarine and pepper. Mix well. Transfer the potatoes to a 10-inch pie plate or quiche dish that has been coated with nonstick cooking spray and bake at 425°F for 25 minutes. Set aside and cool for 10 minutes.

Attach the grating disc to the bowl and feed the ham, green pepper and cheese through the chute. Remove the bowl and add the soup and the eggs. Blend together and pour evenly over the potatoes. Bake at 350°F for 50 minutes. Let stand 10 minutes before serving.

❧ SERVES 8.

Calories:. 132	Carbohydrates: . . . . 14 g.
Total Fat:. . . . . 4 g.	Protein: . . . . 13 g.
Saturated Fat:. . . . . 2 g.	Cholesterol: . . . . 67 mg.
% Calories from Fat: 24	Sodium: . . . . 597 mg.

Green Chile Enchilada Eggplant

1/2 c.	green onions
2 small	eggplants, unpeeled
6 oz.	reduced fat cheddar cheese
1 tbsp.	vegetable oil
15 oz.	can tomato sauce
2 4 oz.	cans chopped green chiles, drained
2 1/4 oz.	can sliced olives, drained
1/2 tsp.	ground cumin
1/4 tsp.	hot pepper sauce
1/4 tsp.	garlic powder
2 cups	baked tortilla chips, crushed
1/2 c.	nonfat sour cream

Attach the slicing disc to the main body of the saladXPRESS™ and fasten it to the bowl, securing the safety latches. Use the slice/grate function and feed the green onions through the chute. Cut into thin slices. Repeat the process with the eggplants, slicing each 1/2-inch thick. Remove the vegetables from the bowl and set aside. Attach the grating disc and shred the cheese.

Preheat the oven to 450°F. Brush both sides of the eggplants with oil and place them on a baking sheet. Bake for 15 minutes until the eggplant is tender. In a medium saucepan over medium-high heat, combine the green onions, tomato sauce, green chiles, olives, cumin, hot pepper sauce and the garlic powder. Bring to a boil, cover, reduce the heat and simmer 10 minutes.

Reduce the oven to 350°F. Arrange half of the eggplant in a 2-quart casserole that has been coated with nonstick cooking spray. Spoon half of the tomato sauce over the eggplant and layer half of the cheese over the eggplant. Repeat the layers. Top with the crushed tortilla chips. Bake, uncovered, for 20 to 30 minutes, until the dish is warmed throughout. Serve with the sour cream.

✍ SERVES 6.

Calories: *335*	*Carbohydrates:* . . . . *53 g.*
Total Fat: . . . . *11 g.*	*Protein:* . . . . *16 g.*
Saturated Fat: . . . . *2 g.*	*Cholesterol:* . . . . *33 mg.*
% Calories from Fat: *37*	*Sodium:* . . . . *914 mg.*

Golden Gruyère Cheese Potato Pie

2 large	baking potatoes, peeled
2 oz.	lowfat Gruyère cheese (you may substitute reduced fat cheddar)
2 tbsp.	lowfat margarine, melted
1	egg, lightly beaten (use egg substitute, if desired)
dash	black pepper
2 tsp.	fresh Italian parsley, minced
2 tbsp.	all-purpose flour
1/2 tsp.	paprika

Attach the grating disc to the main body of the saladXPRESS™ and fasten it to the bowl, securing the safety latches. Use the slice/grate function and feed the potatoes through the chute. Remove the shredded potatoes, rinse and drain well. Use paper towels to absorb any excess moisture and set aside. Shred the Gruyère cheese using the saladXPRESS™ and set aside.

Preheat the oven to 400°F. In a medium bowl, combine the shredded potatoes, egg, pepper and the fresh parsley thoroughly. Add the flour and stir well. Firmly press the potato pie into a 9-inch pie plate that has been coated with nonstick cooking spray. Sprinkle the cheese on top of the potatoes and then sprinkle with the paprika. Bake for 35 to 40 minutes, or until golden brown. Cut into wedges and serve.

 SERVES. 4.

Calories:. 133	Carbohydrates: . . . . 13 g.
Total Fat:. . . . . 5 g.	Protein: . . . . 10 g.
Saturated Fat:. . . . . 4 g.	Cholesterol: . . . . 69 mg.
% Calories from Fat: 42	Sodium: . . . . 468 mg.

Balsamic Roasted Carrots & Peppers

2 lbs.	carrots, peeled
2 each	red and green bell peppers, seeded
1 medium	yellow onion, peeled and quartered
1 clove	garlic
1 tbsp.	extra virgin olive oil
1 tbsp.	balsamic vinegar
1 tbsp.	fresh Italian parsley, minced
1/2 tsp.	salt
1/4 tsp.	black pepper

Attach the slicing disc to the main body of the saladXPRESS™ and fasten it to the bowl, securing the safety latches. Use the slice/grate function and feed the carrots through the chute. Slice the bell peppers. Attach the grating disc and grate the onion and garlic.

Preheat the oven to 475°F. In a 9" x 13" baking pan that has been coated with nonstick cooking spray, combine the carrots, bell peppers, onion, garlic and olive oil. Bake uncovered until the carrots begin to brown around the edges, about 15 minutes. Add the vinegar, parsley, salt and pepper and stir to mix. Continue to bake and turn frequently until the carrots are glazed a dark brown, about 1 hour.

SERVES 6.

Calories:. 118	Carbohydrates: . . . . 23 g.
Total Fat:. . . . . 3 g.	Protein:. . . . . 3 g.
Saturated Fat:. . . . . <1 g.	Cholesterol: . . . . 0 mg.
% Calories from Fat: 20	Sodium: . . . . 249 mg.

Italian Vegetable Pasta Primavera

1 medium	carrot, scraped
1 small	red bell pepper, seeded
1 small	green bell pepper, seeded
1 medium	zucchini, ends removed
2	Roma tomatoes, seeded
3 oz.	Parmesan cheese
1 tsp.	extra virgin olive oil
1/2 cup	broccoli florets
1/4 cup	frozen petite peas
1/4 lb.	fresh asparagus spear tips
6 oz.	rigatoni pasta, cooked al dente and drained
2 tbsp.	fresh Italian parsley, chopped
1 tbsp.	lemon juice
1/2 tsp.	salt
1/8 tsp.	black pepper

Attach the slicing disc to the main body of the saladXPRESS™ and fasten it to the bowl, securing the safety latches. Use the slice/grate function and feed the carrot through the chute. Slice the carrot pieces 1/4-inch thick. Repeat the process with the bell peppers, zucchini and the tomatoes. Spoon the vegetables into a separate bowl. Attach the grating disc and grate the Parmesan cheese. Set aside.

In a large sauté pan over medium heat, sauté the sliced vegetables and broccoli florets in 1 teaspoon of olive oil until the vegetables are just tender. Add the peas and the asparagus and sauté an additional

2 minutes. Place the cooked pasta in a serving bowl, add the sautéed vegetables, Parmesan cheese, parsley, lemon juice, salt and black pepper. Toss gently to mix.

✍ SERVES 4.

Calories: *210*	*Carbohydrates:* . . . . *24 g.*
Total Fat: . . . . *7 g.*	*Protein:* . . . . *14 g.*
Saturated Fat: . . . . *<1 g.*	*Cholesterol:* . . . . *14 mg.*
% Calories from Fat: *29*	*Sodium:* . . . . *655 mg.*

Chipotle Chile Sautéed Tomatoes

1	dried chipotle pepper, stemmed and seeded
2 tbsp.	extra virgin olive oil, divided
15	plum tomatoes, cored
1 small	white onion, peeled
1 clove	garlic
	salt and pepper to taste
dash	red vinegar
2 tbsp.	fresh cilantro, chopped

Cover the pepper with boiling water and soak for 10 minutes. Remove the pepper and finely chop. Mix together the chipotle pepper and 1 tablespoon of the oil in a sealable plastic bag. Attach the slicing disc to the main body of the saladXPRESS™ and fasten it to the bowl, securing the safety latches. Use the slice/grate function and feed the tomatoes through the chute. Slice the tomatoes into 1/2-inch thick slices. Place the tomato slices in the chipotle marinade and refrigerate for 1 hour.

Attach the slicing disc to the main body of the saladXPRESS™ and cut the onion and garlic. In a sauté pan over medium heat, cook the onion and garlic in the remaining olive oil until they are just soft. Increase the heat to medium-high and add the tomatoes to the pan. Sauté until the tomatoes are seared on both sides. Add any remaining marinade, salt, pepper, vinegar and the cilantro. Continue cooking for 1 minute and serve.

SERVES 4 TO 5.

Calories: 98	*Carbohydrates:* . . . . 10 g.
Total Fat: . . . . 6 g.	*Protein:* . . . . 2 g.
Saturated Fat: . . . . <1 g.	*Cholesterol:* . . . . 0 mg.
% Calories from Fat: 54	*Sodium:* . . . . 49 mg.

Creamy Asiago Potatoes

1 medium	white onion, peeled and quartered
1 clove	garlic
1 1/4 lbs.	baking potatoes, peeled and quartered
4 oz.	reduced fat Asiago cheese
1 tsp.	extra virgin olive oil
1	bay leaf
dash	ground nutmeg
1/2 tsp.	black pepper
3/4 cup	evaporated milk
1/4 cup	lowfat milk
1/2 cup	plain dry bread crumbs
1 tbsp.	extra virgin olive oil
1 tbsp.	fresh parsley, chopped

Attach the slicing disc to the main body of the saladXPRESS™ and fasten it to the bowl, securing the safety latches. Use the slice/grate function and feed the onion and garlic through the chute. Thinly slice the onion and garlic, and set them aside in a separate bowl. Repeat the process with the potatoes, slicing them into 1/8-inch thickness. Place them in a large bowl and set aside. Attach the grating disc and grate the Asiago cheese.

Preheat the oven to 400°F. In a large sauté pan, cook the onion and garlic in the oil until tender. Add the bay leaf, nutmeg and 1/4-teaspoon pepper. Stir to combine and add the evaporated milk and lowfat milk. Bring just to a boil and remove from the heat. Cover and let it stand for 5 minutes. In a separate bowl, combine the Asiago cheese and the bread crumbs. Toss with the olive oil, parsley and the remaining pepper.

Remove the bay leaf from the milk sauce and discard. Add the sauce to the potatoes, tossing gently. Layer half of the potatoes into a 2-quart baking pan that has been coated with nonstick cooking spray. Top with half of the cheese/bread crumb mixture. Repeat the layers. Cover and bake for 60 minutes, or until the potatoes are tender. Just before serving, uncover and bake for a few minutes to crisp the cheese and bread topping.

~&~ SERVES 4.

Calories:. 260	Carbohydrates: . . . . 21 g.
Total Fat: . . . . 15 g.	Protein: . . . . 15 g.
Saturated Fat:. . . . . 2 g.	Cholesterol: . . . . 15 mg.
% Calories from Fat: 30	Sodium: . . . . 501 mg.

Sun-Dried Tomato Pesto Roasted Vegetables

2 cups	red potatoes
2 cups	zucchini
1 1/2 cups	red onions
2 cups	eggplant
2 tbsp.	red vinegar
1 tbsp.	extra virgin olive oil
dash	salt
dash	black pepper
3 tbsp.	prepared sun-dried tomato pesto

Attach the slicing disc to the main body of the saladXPRESS™ and fasten it to the bowl, securing the safety latches. Use the slice/grate function and feed the potatoes through the chute. Cut into 1/2-inch slices. Repeat the process for the zucchini, onions and eggplant. Combine all of the vegetables in the bowl and add the vinegar, olive oil, salt and pepper and toss. Let stand for 3 minutes.

Preheat the oven to 475°F. Lightly spray a jelly roll pan with nonstick cooking spray. Place the vegetables in a single layer on the pan and bake for 10 minutes. Turn the vegetables and bake an additional 10 minutes. Roast any remaining vegetables in batches as directed above. In a wide serving bowl, gently toss the roasted vegetables with the pesto and serve.

~ SERVES 4.

Calories:. 121	Carbohydrates: . . . . 17 g.
Total Fat:. . . . . 5 g.	Protein:. . . . . 5 g.
Saturated Fat:. . . . . <1 g.	Cholesterol: . . . . 0 mg.
% Calories from Fat: 33	Sodium: . . . . 151 mg.

Golden Potato & Spinach Patties

2 medium	baking potatoes, peeled
3	carrots, scraped
1/4	head lettuce
1/2	onion, peeled and cut in half
2 cups	fresh spinach
2	eggs, lightly beaten (use egg substitute, if desired)
1 cup	all-purpose flour
1 tsp.	baking powder
1/8 tsp.	black pepper
1/8 tsp.	paprika
1 tbsp.	fresh parsley, minced

Attach the grating disc to the main body of the saladXPRESS™ and fasten it to the bowl, securing the safety latches. Use the slice/grate function and feed the potatoes through the chute. Repeat the process with the carrots, lettuce, onion and spinach. Add the eggs, mixing well. In a small bowl combine the flour, baking powder, pepper, paprika and parsley. Add to the vegetables and toss again.

Using a nonstick sauté pan on medium heat, spoon 1/4-cup batter into the pan. Spread the batter into a 4-inch circle and brown on both sides. Serve immediately.

SERVES 4 TO 5.

Calories:. 175	Carbohydrates: . . . . 31 g.
Total Fat:. . . . . 2 g.	Protein:. . . . . 8 g.
Saturated Fat:. . . . . <1 g.	Cholesterol: . . . . 85 mg.
% Calories from Fat: 13	Sodium: . . . . 373 mg.

Herbed Vegetables in Polenta

2 cups	potatoes, peeled
1 small	white onion,
5	Roma tomatoes
2 tbsp.	lowfat margarine
2 cloves	garlic
2 tsp.	all-purpose flour
1/4 tsp.	black pepper
2 tsp.	fresh thyme, minced
2 cups	fresh or frozen, thawed peas
1 lb.	prepared polenta, cut into 1-inch thick slices
1/2 tsp.	paprika

Attach the slicing disc to the main body of the saladXPRESS™ and fasten it to the bowl, securing the safety latches. Use the slice/grate function and feed the potatoes through the chute. Repeat the process with the onion and tomatoes. In a small saucepan over low heat, melt the margarine. Press the garlic and add it to the margarine. Stir in the flour, pepper and fresh thyme. Set aside.

Preheat the oven to 350°F. Layer the peas in the bottom of a 2-quart baking dish that has been coated with nonstick cooking spray. Dot a bit of the herbed flour over the peas. Layer the potatoes and onions over the peas, topping each with a bit of the herbed flour. Place the tomato slices on top and top with any remaining herbed flour over all. Cover tightly and bake for 30 minutes.

Uncover the vegetables, top with the polenta rounds, sprinkle with the paprika and continue baking, uncovered, for 30 minutes.

◆ SERVES 4 TO 5.

Calories: *301*	*Carbohydrates:* . . . . *53 g.*
Total Fat: . . . . *6 g.*	*Protein:* . . . . *12 g.*
Saturated Fat: . . . . *2 g.*	*Cholesterol:* . . . . *4 mg.*
% Calories from Fat: *17*	*Sodium:* . . . . *558 mg.*

Herbed Red Potato Puff

4 medium	red potatoes, scrubbed
8 oz.	reduced fat cheddar cheese
1/4 cup	reduced fat Swiss cheese
8 oz.	very lean ham
3	eggs (use egg substitute, if desired)
1 cup	nonfat milk
1/4 tsp.	salt
1 tsp.	fresh parsley, minced
1 tsp.	fresh dill, minced

Attach the grating disc to the main body of the saladXPRESS™ and fasten it to the bowl, securing the safety latches. Use the slice/grate function and feed the potatoes through the chute. Repeat the process with both cheeses. Grate the ham and place in a separate bowl.

Press the grated potatoes into a 9-inch pie plate that has been coated with nonstick cooking spray. Coat the top of the potatoes with the cooking spray. Bake the potato crust in the oven at 425°F for 25 minutes. Layer the cheeses and ham over the potatoes.

Reduce the oven temperature to 350°F. In a separate bowl, beat together the eggs, milk, salt, parsley and dill. Pour over the ham and cheese and bake for 30 to 40 minutes. When done, the puff will be set and golden.

⮞ SERVES 4.

Calories:. 324	Carbohydrates: . . . . 17 g.
Total Fat: . . . . 11 g.	Protein: . . . . 41 g.
Saturated Fat:. . . . . 5 g.	Cholesterol:. . . . . 193 mg.
% Calories from Fat: 30	Sodium: . . . . 1203 mg.

Buttery Summer Squash Patties

2 cups	summer squash
1/4	yellow onion
3 oz.	lowfat cheddar cheese
1/2 cup	prepared lowfat baking mix
1 tsp.	fresh parsley, minced
1/2 tsp.	salt
1/4 tsp.	black pepper
2	eggs, lightly beaten (use egg substitute, if desired)
2 tbsp.	lowfat margarine

Attach the grating disc to the main body of the saladXPRESS™ and fasten it to the bowl, securing the safety latches. Use the slice/grate function and feed the squash through the chute. Repeat with the onion and the cheddar cheese. Add the baking mix, parsley, salt, pepper and the eggs to the bowl and toss well. Form the squash batter into 6 patties. In a heavy skillet over medium heat, fry the patties in the margarine until lightly browned on each side, about 4 to 6 minutes per side.

SERVES 6.

Calories:. 142	Carbohydrates: . . . . 12 g.
Total Fat:. . . . . 6 g.	Protein: . . . . 11 g.
Saturated Fat:. . . . . 2 g.	Cholesterol:. . . . . 108 mg.
% Calories from Fat: 38	Sodium: . . . . 661 mg.

Spicy Hot Hash Browns

4	russet potatoes, peeled and quartered
16 oz.	reduced fat lean ham
1/2	purple onion, peeled and cut in half
1	green bell pepper, seeded
1	fresh jalapeño chile, seeded
1 tbsp.	lowfat margarine
1 tsp.	black pepper
1/4 tsp.	cayenne pepper
1/2 tsp.	paprika
4 oz.	reduced fat cheddar cheese

Attach the grating disc to the main body of the saladXPRESS™ and fasten it to the bowl, securing the safety latches. Use the slice/grate function and feed the potatoes through the chute. Remove the bowl and transfer the potatoes to a mixing bowl.

Reattach the grating disc and feed the ham, onion, bell pepper and chile through the chute. Heat the oil in a large sauté pan and add the ham, onion, pepper and chile. Cook until the vegetables are softened. Cool for 10 minutes and add to the grated potatoes. Add the pepper, cayenne and paprika to the ham and vegetables and mix well.

Heat a nonstick griddle or large sauté pan and coat with nonstick cooking spray. Drop the potatoes by large spoonfuls and flatten to form patties. Coat the patties with cooking spray and cook for 5 minutes. Turn and spray the other side of each patty and continue cooking until golden on both sides. Attach the grating disc to the saladXPRESS™ and grate the cheese. To serve, top each patty with a bit of grated cheese.

◆ SERVES 6.

Calories: *198*	*Carbohydrates:* . . . . *19 g.*
Total Fat: . . . . *4 g.*	*Protein:* . . . . *24 g.*
Saturated Fat: . . . . *2 g.*	*Cholesterol:* . . . . *29 mg.*
% Calories from Fat: *18*	*Sodium:* . . . . *833 mg.*

Chapter 4

Soups
& Salads

Kowloon Bay Chicken & Bok Choy Soup

1 large	boneless, skinless chicken breast, cooked
2 cloves	garlic
1/2-inch piece	fresh ginger, peeled
2 cups	bok choy, woody stems removed, washed and spin-dried
2	Roma tomatoes, seeded
1/2 cup	canned water chestnuts
4	green onions
1 tsp.	sesame oil
13.5 oz.	can lowfat coconut milk
15 oz.	nonfat chicken broth
1/2 tsp.	salt
1/2 tsp.	black pepper
1 tbsp.	fresh cilantro, minced

Attach the slicing disc to the main body of the saladXPRESS™ and fasten it to the bowl, securing the safety latches. Use the slice/grate function and feed the chicken through the chute. Repeat the process with the garlic, ginger, bok choy, tomatoes, water chestnuts and onions.

Spoon the chicken and vegetables into a large saucepan. Add the oil, toss and cook for 3 to 5 minutes on medium-high heat. Add the coconut milk, chicken broth, salt and pepper and cook on medium heat until steaming. Garnish with the cilantro to serve.

∾ SERVES 4.

Calories:. 175	Carbohydrates: . . . . 9 g.
Total Fat:. . . . . 12 g.	Protein:. . . . . 8 g.
Saturated Fat:. . . . . 6 g.	Cholesterol: . . . . 16 mg.
% Calories from Fat: 61	Sodium:. . . . . 519 mg.

East Indian Black Bean Soup

1 large	yellow onion, peeled
3 cloves	garlic
4	ripe tomatoes, seeded
1	green bell pepper, seeded
2	carrots, peeled
1 tsp.	liquid smoke
2 cups	canned black beans, drained
1/2 tsp.	ground cumin
1/4 tsp.	ground allspice
1/2 tsp.	ground coriander
2 tbsp.	fresh parsley, minced
4 cups	water
4 cups	nonfat chicken broth
	salt and pepper to taste

Attach the slicing disc to the main body of the saladXPRESS™ and fasten it to the bowl, securing the safety latches. Use the slice/grate function and feed the onion through the chute. Repeat the process with the garlic, tomatoes, green bell pepper and carrots. Place all of the vegetables in a stockpot and add the liquid smoke, beans, spices and parsley. Add the water and chicken broth and heat on medium until the soup is bubbling and the vegetables are tender. Season with the salt and pepper to taste.

◆ SERVES 6.

Calories:. 124	Carbohydrates: . . . . 25 g.
Total Fat: . . . . <1 g.	Protein: . . . . 8 g.
Saturated Fat: . . . . <1 g.	Cholesterol: . . . . 3 mg.
% Calories from Fat: 5	Sodium: . . . . 616 mg.

Hearty Winter Split Pea Soup

1/2	white onion, peeled and cut in half
6 large	carrots, peeled
2	baking potatoes, peeled and quartered
1 1/2 cups	split peas
8 cups	nonfat chicken broth
1 tbsp.	fresh tarragon, minced
1 tbsp.	fresh parsley, minced
1 tsp.	white pepper
1/2 tsp.	salt

Attach the slicing disc to the main body of the saladXPRESS™ and fasten it to the bowl, securing the safety latches. Use the slice/grate function and feed the onion through the chute. Repeat the process with the carrots and potatoes.

Place the vegetables in a large stockpot and add the peas and chicken broth. Mix well and add the tarragon, parsley, pepper and salt. Cook on medium heat for 40 to 50 minutes, or until the peas and potatoes are very tender. Remove from the stockpot and puree the hot soup in a blender. Serve while hot.

✎ SERVES 8.

Calories:. 194		Carbohydrates: . . . . 35 g.
Total Fat: . . . . <1 g.		Protein: . . . . 14 g.
Saturated Fat: . . . . <1 g.		Cholesterol: . . . . 5 mg.
% Calories from Fat: 3		Sodium: . . . . 567 mg.

Fresh Mushroom, Spinach & Chive Soup

1/2 lb.	fresh white mushrooms, scrubbed and stems removed
1/2 bunch	chives, washed
2 bunches	fresh spinach, stems removed, washed and spin-dried
4 cups	nonfat chicken broth
2 tbsp.	lemon juice
1/4 cup	rice vinegar
1/2 tsp.	black pepper
1/4 tsp.	salt

Attach the slicing disc to the main body of the saladXPRESS™ and fasten it to the bowl, securing the safety latches. Use the slice/grate function and feed the mushrooms through the chute. Repeat the process with the chives and spinach.

Place the vegetables in a large stockpot and add the chicken broth, lemon juice, vinegar, pepper and salt. Cook on medium heat until the spinach and mushrooms are tender.

SERVES 6.

Calories: 36	Carbohydrates: . . . . 4 g.
Total Fat: . . . . <1 g.	Protein: . . . . 3 g.
Saturated Fat: . . . . <1 g.	Cholesterol: . . . . 3 mg.
% Calories from Fat: 5	Sodium: . . . . 367 mg.

Fresh Minestrone

1 large	onion, peeled and quartered
2 cloves	garlic, peeled
2 medium	carrots, peeled
2 ribs	celery
1 cup	fresh green beans
2 tbsp.	extra virgin olive oil
16 oz.	can diced tomatoes
1 cup	tomato sauce
1	bay leaf
1 tsp.	dried basil
1 tsp.	dried oregano
1 sprig	fresh parsley
2/3 cup	orzo pasta, cooked al dente and drained
16 oz.	can chickpeas, drained and rinsed
	salt and pepper to taste

Attach the slicing disc to the main body of the saladXPRESS™ and fasten it to the bowl, securing the safety latches. Use the slice/grate function and feed the onion through the chute. Repeat the process with the garlic, carrots, celery and green beans. Heat the oil in a large soup pot and sauté the onion and garlic over medium heat until golden. Add the carrots, celery and green beans. Add just enough water to cover and stir. Add the tomatoes, tomato sauce and bay leaf, basil and oregano. Simmer, covered for 50 to 60 minutes.

Using the slicing disc, slice the fresh parsley in the saladXPRESS™.

Add the cooked orzo, chickpeas and parsley to the soup. Add more water if needed, and salt and pepper to taste. Simmer on low heat for 5 minutes, remove the bay leaf and serve.

❧ SERVES 8.

Calories:. 166	Carbohydrates: . . . . 27 g.
Total Fat:. . . . . 3 g.	Protein:. . . . . 7 g.
Saturated Fat:. . . . . <1 g.	Cholesterol: . . . . 3 mg.
% Calories from Fat: 18	Sodium: . . . . 529 mg.

Early Spring Asparagus Soup

2 large	boneless, skinless chicken breasts, cooked
4	green onions
2 cloves	garlic
4 ribs	celery
1 lb.	fresh asparagus, tough woody stems removed
3 1/2 cups	nonfat chicken broth
1/4 tsp.	cayenne pepper
1 tbsp.	all-purpose flour
1/3 cup	hot water
1 tbsp.	fresh parsley, minced
1/2 tsp.	salt
1 tsp.	white pepper
2 oz.	uncooked ziti pasta

Attach the slicing disc to the main body of the saladXPRESS™ and fasten it to the bowl, securing the safety latches. Use the slice/grate function and feed the chicken through the chute. Repeat the process with the onions, garlic, celery and asparagus.

Place the chicken and vegetables in a large stockpot and add the broth and cayenne. Heat on medium-high until the broth is boiling. Mix together in a small bowl the flour and hot water until smooth and add to the boiling broth. Reduce the heat to low and stir until thickened. Add the parsley, salt, pepper and pasta and cook on low until the pasta is tender and the vegetables are cooked through.

⮞ SERVES 6.

Calories:.	141	Carbohydrates:	15 g.
Total Fat:.	3 g.	Protein:	11 g.
Saturated Fat:.	<1 g.	Cholesterol:	21 mg.
% Calories from Fat:	19	Sodium:.	449 mg.

Balsamic Mushroom & Pepper Salad

1	red bell pepper, seeded
1	yellow bell pepper, seeded
1	cucumber, peeled
1 large	purple onion, cut into large pieces
20	crimini mushrooms, scrubbed and trimmed
20	cherry tomatoes
2 tbsp.	extra virgin olive oil
2 tbsp.	balsamic vinegar
3 tbsp.	water
1 tsp.	freshly ground black pepper
1/2 tsp.	salt

Attach the slicing disc to the main body of the saladXPRESS™ and fasten it to the bowl, securing the safety latches. Use the slice/grate function and feed the red bell pepper through the chute. Repeat the process with the yellow bell pepper, cucumber, onion and mushrooms. Add the tomatoes to the sliced vegetables. Toss until well blended.

In a separate bowl, whisk together the oil, vinegar, water, pepper and salt. Pour the dressing over the vegetables and toss again. Cover and refrigerate for at least 1 hour. Present the salad in the serving bowl.

SERVES 4.

Calories: 157	Carbohydrates: . . . . 19 g.
Total Fat: . . . . 8 g.	Protein: . . . . 5 g.
Saturated Fat: . . . . 1 g.	Cholesterol: . . . . 0 mg.
% Calories from Fat: 42	Sodium: . . . . 306 mg.

Turkey Salad with Spicy Pear & Apple Chutney

1 1/4 lbs.	turkey tenderloin
1/2	cantaloupe, peeled and roughly cut
2 cups	red seedless grapes
1 rib	celery
1/4 cup	lowfat mayonnaise
2 tbsp.	nonfat milk
1/2 cup	Spicy Pear & Apple Chutney (see p. 26)
2 tbsp.	cider vinegar
1 tbsp.	brown sugar
1 head	romaine lettuce, washed and spin-dried
1 tbsp.	toasted coconut, grated
1 tbsp.	raisins
1 tbsp.	green onions, sliced

Coat a large nonstick sauté pan with cooking spray and add the turkey. Cook over medium heat for 5 to 6 minutes on each side, or until no pink remains. Slice thinly.

Attach the slicing disc to the main body of the saladXPRESS™ and fasten it to the bowl, securing the safety latches. Use the slice/grate function and feed the cantaloupe through the chute. Repeat the process with the grapes and celery. Remove the bowl and add in the turkey and mix.

In a separate bowl, mix together the mayonnaise, milk, chutney, vinegar and brown sugar. Whisk until well blended. Drizzle the dressing over the salad and blend well. Serve over romaine leaves and top with the coconut, raisins and green onions.

❦ SERVES 6.

Calories: *279*	*Carbohydrates:* . . . . *74 g.*
Total Fat: . . . . *4 g.*	*Protein:* . . . . *26 g.*
Saturated Fat: . . . . *<1 g.*	*Cholesterol:* . . . . *59 mg.*
% Calories from Fat: *8*	*Sodium:* . . . . *378 mg.*

Dijon Mustard Slim Slaw

1 head	green cabbage, washed and cored
1 head	purple cabbage, washed and cored
2 medium	carrots, peeled
1/2	white onion
1	red bell pepper, seeded
2 sprigs	fresh parsley
2 tsp.	Dijon mustard
1/2 cup	lowfat mayonnaise
1 tbsp.	vegetable oil
1/2 tsp.	salt
1 tsp.	black pepper

Attach the grating disc to the main body of the saladXPRESS™ and fasten it to the bowl, securing the safety latches. Use the slice/grate function and feed the green cabbage through the chute. Repeat the process with the purple cabbage, carrots, onion, red bell pepper and parsley leaves. Toss the vegetables to blend.

In a separate bowl, whisk together the mustard, mayonnaise, oil, salt and pepper. Pour the dressing over the vegetables and toss again until well blended. Cover and refrigerate in the serving bowl for 1 hour.

❧ SERVES 8.

Calories:. 136	Carbohydrates: . . . . 25 g.
Total Fat:. . . . . 4 g.	Protein:. . . . . 5 g.
Saturated Fat:. . . . . <1 g.	Cholesterol: . . . . <1 mg.
% Calories from Fat: 22	Sodium:. . . . . 355 mg.

Fruit Salad with Creamy Poppy Seed Dressing

1 medium	apple, cored
1	seedless orange, peeled and sectioned
1	kiwi, peeled
1	nectarine, pitted and cut in half
1 cup	strawberries, hulled
1/2 cup	blueberries
1/2 cup	raspberries

Poppy Seed Dressing:

2 tbsp.	nonfat vanilla yogurt
1 tbsp.	honey
1 tbsp.	frozen limeade concentrate, thawed
2 tsp.	vegetable oil
1/4 tsp.	poppy seeds
1/2 tsp.	dry mustard

Attach the slicing disc to the main body of the saladXPRESS™ and fasten it to the bowl, securing the safety latches. Use the slice/grate function and feed the apple through the chute. Repeat the process with the orange, kiwi, nectarine and strawberries. Remove the bowl and add the blueberries and raspberries. Mix well and set aside.

In a separate bowl, combine the yogurt, honey, limeade, oil, poppy seed and mustard. Blend well. Drizzle over the fruit and stir carefully.

❧ SERVES 6.

Calories:. 112		Carbohydrates: . . . . 56 g.	
Total Fat:. . . . . 4 g.		Protein:. . . . . 5 g.	
Saturated Fat:. . . . . 2 g.		Cholesterol: . . . . 8 mg.	
% Calories from Fat: 26		Sodium:. . . . . 52 mg.	

Crisp Green Salad with Herb Vinaigrette

2 ribs	celery
4	radishes, cleaned and ends removed
3	plum tomatoes
1/2 small	purple onion, peeled
1/2 cup	frozen peas, thawed and drained
10	romaine lettuce leaves, washed and spin-dried, torn
1 tbsp.	extra virgin olive oil
2 tbsp.	balsamic vinegar
1 tbsp.	fresh parsley, minced
1 tsp.	fresh thyme, minced
1 tsp.	fresh rosemary, minced
2 tbsp.	water
1 tsp.	garlic powder
1/2 tsp.	salt
1 tsp.	black pepper

Attach the slicing disc to the main body of the saladXPRESS™ and fasten it to the bowl, securing the safety latches. Use the slice/grate function and feed the celery through the chute. Repeat the process with the radishes, tomatoes and onion. Remove the bowl and add in the frozen peas and prepared lettuce. Toss to blend and cover and refrigerate for 1 hour.

In a separate bowl, combine the oil, vinegar, herbs, water, garlic powder, salt and pepper. Whisk until well blended. Pour the vinaigrette over the crisp salad and toss to coat. Serve while chilled.

SERVES 6.

Calories: 55	Carbohydrates: . . . . 7 g.
Total Fat: . . . . 3 g.	Protein: . . . . 2 g.
Saturated Fat: . . . . <1 g.	Cholesterol: . . . . 0 mg.
% Calories from Fat: 41	Sodium: . . . . 232 mg.

Gorgonzola Cheese & Walnut Potato Salad

3 lbs.	red potatoes, cut in half and steamed until slightly soft
2	green onions
1 sprig	parsley
6	walnuts, chopped
1/4 cup	gorgonzola cheese, crumbled

Creamy Dressing:

1 cup	nonfat plain yogurt
1 tbsp.	sugar
1/4 cup	nonfat milk
1/2 tsp.	dry mustard
	salt and pepper to taste

Attach the slicing disc to the main body of the saladXPRESS™ and fasten it to the bowl, securing the safety latches. Use the slice/grate function and feed the potatoes through the chute. Repeat the process with the onions and parsley. Remove the bowl and add the walnuts and cheese and toss gently.

In a seperate bowl, combine the yogurt, sugar, milk, mustard, salt and pepper. Mix well and pour over the salad. Toss to coat. Cover and refrigerate for at least 2 hours.

SERVES 8.

Calories: 96	Carbohydrates: . . . . 14 g.
Total Fat: . . . . 2 g.	Protein: . . . . 6 g.
Saturated Fat: . . . . <1 g.	Cholesterol: . . . . 5 mg.
% Calories from Fat: 21	Sodium: . . . . 94 mg.

Caribbean Salad with Tomato Orange Dressing

2	boneless, skinless chicken breasts, cooked
1	papaya, peeled and seeded
1	mango, peeled
1/2 medium	purple onion, peeled and cut in half
1	red bell pepper, seeded
2	plum tomatoes

Tomato Orange Dressing:

3	ripe tomatoes, peeled
1/2 cup	orange juice
2 tbsp.	vegetable oil
1 tbsp.	ketchup
1 tbsp.	lemon juice
2 tsp.	orange zest

Attach the slicing disc to the main body of the saladXPRESS™ and fasten it to the bowl, securing the safety latches. Use the slice/grate function and feed the chicken through the chute. Repeat the process with the papaya, mango, onion, red bell pepper and tomatoes. Remove the bowl and transfer the salad to a serving bowl. Mix well.

To make the dressing, place the tomatoes in a blender with the orange juice, oil, ketchup, lemon juice and orange zest. Puree the dressing until creamy. Serve the salad with the dressing on the side.

MAKES 4 SERVINGS.

Calories:. 242	Carbohydrates: . . . . 36 g.
Total Fat:. . . . . 9 g.	Protein: . . . . 12 g.
Saturated Fat:. . . . . 2 g.	Cholesterol: . . . . 28 mg.
% Calories from Fat: 32	Sodium: . . . . 100 mg.

Fruit Salad with Creamy Pineapple Dressing & Pecans

3	seedless oranges, peeled and sectioned
2	red apples, halved and cored
2	bananas, peeled
1 bunch	red grapes, seedless
1 bunch	green grapes, seedless
1 bunch	baby spinach leaves, washed and spin-dried

Creamy Pineapple Dressing:

1 cup	canned crushed pineapple
2/3 cup	plain nonfat yogurt
2 tbsp.	Neufchatel cheese
2 tbsp.	honey
2 tsp.	orange zest
1/4 cup	pecans, shelled

Attach the slicing disc to the main body of the saladXPRESS™ and fasten it to the bowl, securing the safety latches. Use the slice/grate function and feed the oranges through the chute. Repeat the process with the apples and bananas. Remove the bowl and add the red and green grapes and mix well. Add the spinach leaves to the salad.

In a blender, combine the pineapple, yogurt, cheese, honey and orange zest. Pulse until smooth. Blend well and pour over the salad. Toss the salad to coat and garnish with the pecans.

❧ SERVES 6 TO 8.

Calories:. 230	Carbohydrates: . . . . 42 g.
Total Fat:. . . . . 7 g.	Protein:. . . . . 4 g.
Saturated Fat:. . . . . 2 g.	Cholesterol: . . . . 6 mg.
% Calories from Fat: 21	Sodium:. . . . . 49 mg.

Homestyle Cobb Salad

3 large	carrots, peeled
1 medium	cucumber, peeled
3 ribs	celery
6 leaves	romaine lettuce, washed and spin-dried, torn
1	boneless, skinless turkey breast, cooked
1/2 cup	cherry tomatoes, halved
1 cup	lowfat blue cheese, crumbled
1	hard cooked egg, chopped
4 slices	turkey bacon, cooked and crumbled
	bottled lowfat herb vinaigrette

Attach the slicing disc to the main body of the saladXPRESS™ and fasten it to the bowl, securing the safety latches. Use the slice/grate function and feed the carrots through the chute. Repeat the process with the cucumber, celery, lettuce and turkey breast. Remove the bowl and add in the cherry tomatoes. Toss.

To assemble the salads, place equal amounts of the turkey and vegetables on 4 plates. Layer the blue cheese, egg and bacon over each salad. Drizzle the vinaigrette lightly over each salad to serve.

MAKES 4 SERVINGS.

Calories:. 244	Carbohydrates: . . . . 11 g.
Total Fat: . . . . 15 g.	Protein: . . . . 19 g.
Saturated Fat:. . . . . 8 g.	Cholesterol:. . . . . 101 mg.
% Calories from Fat: 52	Sodium. . . . . 1017 mg.

Field Greens with Pineapple Sesame Vinaigrette

1 large	boneless, skinless chicken breast, cooked
5	seedless tangelos, peeled
10 cups	mixed field greens, washed and spin-dried
1/4 cup	reduced-fat blue cheese, crumbled
4	walnuts, chopped

Pineapple Sesame Vinaigrette:

2 tbsp.	sesame seeds, toasted
2 tbsp.	sesame oil
1/4 cup	rice vinegar
1/2 cup	pineapple juice

Attach the slicing disc to the main body of the saladXPRESS™ and fasten it to the bowl, securing the safety latches. Use the slice/grate function and feed the chicken through the chute. Repeat the process with the tangelos. Remove the bowl and transfer the chicken and tangelos to a serving bowl. Add the greens and toss.

In a separate bowl, whisk together the sesame seeds, sesame oil, vinegar and pineapple juice. Pour the dressing over the salad and toss to coat. To serve, top with crumbled blue cheese and sprinkle with the walnuts.

MAKES 4 SERVINGS.

Calories: 283	Carbohydrates: . . . . 26 g.
Total Fat: . . . . 17 g.	Protein: . . . . 11 g.
Saturated Fat: . . . . 5 g.	Cholesterol: . . . . 25 mg.
% Calories from Fat: 50	Sodium: . . . . 169 mg.

Mexican Fiesta Salad

1 head	romaine lettuce, washed and spin-dried
4	plum tomatoes
3	green onions
1/2 cup	black olives
1 clove	garlic
1 cup	black beans, drained
1 cup	corn kernels, drained

Fiesta Dressing:

2 tbsp.	prepared margarita mix, without alcohol
2 tbsp.	extra virgin olive oil
2 tbsp.	water
1/2 tsp.	salt
1/2 tsp.	black pepper
1/4 tsp.	chili powder

Attach the slicing disc to the main body of the saladXPRESS™ and fasten it to the bowl, securing the safety latches. Use the slice/grate function and feed the lettuce through the chute. Repeat the process with the tomatoes, onions, olives and garlic. Remove the bowl and add the beans and corn to the salad. Gently toss.

In a separate bowl, combine the margarita mix, oil, water, salt, pepper and chili powder. Whisk together well and drizzle over the salad. Toss to coat.

❧ SERVES 4.

Calories:. 214		Carbohydrates: . . . . 18 g.
Total Fat:. . . . . 7 g.		Protein: . . . . 10 g.
Saturated Fat:. . . . . 1 g.		Cholesterol: . . . . 0 mg.
% Calories from Fat: 20		Sodium: . . . . 609 mg.

Tart & Tangy Potpourri Slaw

1/2 head	green cabbage, cleaned and cored
1/2	yellow onion, peeled and cut in half
2 ribs	celery
1	jalapeño chile, seeded
1 tbsp.	sugar
2 tbsp.	basil vinegar
2 tbsp.	balsamic vinegar
2 tbsp.	rice vinegar
2 tbsp.	red vinegar
2 tsp.	garlic powder
1 tbsp.	honey
1 tbsp.	Worcestershire sauce
1 tsp.	low sodium soy sauce
1 tbsp.	brown mustard seeds, crushed
1 tsp.	black pepper

Attach the slicing disc to the main body of the saladXPRESS™ and fasten it to the bowl, securing the safety latches. Use the slice/grate function and feed the cabbage through the chute. Remove the bowl and transfer the cabbage to a separate bowl filled with water and ice. Refrigerate for 1 hour. Drain well and place the cabbage in a paper towel-lined bowl. Chill for 1 to 2 hours.

Attach the grating disc and grate the onion, celery and jalapeño. Remove the bowl and add the sugar, vinegars, garlic powder, honey, Worcestershire sauce, soy sauce, mustard seeds and pepper. Mix well.

Remove the cabbage from the refrigerator and add it to the other ingredients. Toss to coat. Serve immediately or chill.

❧ SERVES 6.

Calories: 78	Carbohydrates: . . . . 15 g.
Total Fat: . . . . <1 g.	Protein: . . . . 3 g.
Saturated Fat: . . . . <1 g.	Cholesterol: . . . . 0 mg.
% Calories from Fat: 9	Sodium: . . . . 95 mg.

Cilantro Noodle Salad

2	green onions
1 clove	garlic
1 cup	fresh bean sprouts, cleaned
1 sprig	fresh cilantro
2	carrots, peeled
4 oz.	rice vermicelli, cooked al dente and drained

Soy & Pepper Dressing:

2 tbsp.	sesame oil
1 tbsp.	mayonnaise
1/2 cup	plain nonfat yogurt
1/4 tsp.	cayenne pepper
1 tbsp.	rice vinegar
2 tbsp.	soy sauce

Attach the slicing disc to the main body of the saladXPRESS™ and fasten it to the bowl, securing the safety latches. Use the slice/grate function and feed the onions through the chute. Repeat the process with the garlic, bean sprouts, cilantro and carrots. Remove the bowl and set it aside.

In a separate bowl, combine the sesame oil, mayonnaise, yogurt, pepper, vinegar and soy sauce. Whisk together thoroughly. To present the salads, place equal portions of the vermicelli on 4 plates. Top with the vegetables and pour the dressing over each serving.

❦ MAKES 4 SERVINGS.

Calories:. 234	Carbohydrates: . . . . 30 g.
Total Fat: . . . . 10 g.	Protein: . . . . 5 g.
Saturated Fat:. . . . . <1 g.	Cholesterol: . . . . 3 mg.
% Calories from Fat: 39	Sodium: . . . . 517 mg.

Country Cole Slaw

1/2 small	head cabbage, washed and cored
2	carrots, peeled
1 small	green bell pepper, seeded
2	green onions
1/4 cup	lowfat mayonnaise
1 tbsp.	sugar
2 tbsp.	cider vinegar
1/4 tsp.	salt
1/2 tsp.	Dijon mustard
1/8 tsp.	celery seeds

Attach the slicing disc to the main body of the saladXPRESS™ and fasten it to the bowl, securing the safety latches. Use the slice/grate function and feed the cabbage through the chute. Repeat the process with the carrots, green bell pepper and onions. Remove the bowl and set aside.

In a separate bowl, combine the mayonnaise, sugar, vinegar, salt, mustard and celery seeds. Whisk and add to the salad. Toss to coat.

SERVES 6.

Calories: 66	Carbohydrates: . . . . 15 g.
Total Fat:. . . . . 1 g.	Protein:. . . . . 2 g.
Saturated Fat:. . . . . <1 g.	Cholesterol: . . . . <1 mg.
% Calories from Fat: 12	Sodium:. . . . . 220 mg.

Hawaiian Pineapple Coleslaw

1/2 small	head cabbage
2	carrots, peeled
1/2	fresh pineapple, peeled and sectioned
1/2 cup	lowfat mayonnaise
1/2 cup	fat-free plain yogurt
2 tsp.	honey
1	banana, peeled
1/2 cup	pecans, halved

Attach the grating disc to the main body of the saladXPRESS™ and fasten it to the bowl, securing the safety latches. Use the slice/grate function and feed the cabbage through the chute. Repeat the process with the carrots and pineapple. Remove the bowl and set aside.

In a separate bowl, combine the mayonnaise, yogurt and honey. Blend well and pour over the salad. Toss to coat. Refrigerate for at least 1 hour. Attach the slicing disc to the saladXPRESS™ and slice the banana. Attach the grating disc and grate the pecans. To serve, top the salad with the sliced bananas and pecans.

⤹ SERVES 4.

Calories:. 283	Carbohydrates: . . . . 42 g.
Total Fat: . . . . 13 g.	Protein: . . . . 6 g.
Saturated Fat: . . . . <1 g.	Cholesterol: . . . . 1 mg.
% Calories from Fat: 37	Sodium: . . . . 340 mg.

Caraway & Ricotta Cole Slaw

1 head	green cabbage, washed and cored
1 small	green bell pepper
1	apple, cored
1 cup	lowfat ricotta cheese
1/4 cup	lowfat mayonnaise
3 tbsp.	vinegar
1/2 tsp.	salt
1/2 tsp.	caraway seed
1	chive, finely minced

Attach the slicing disc to the main body of the saladXPRESS™ and fasten it to the bowl, securing the safety latches. Use the slice/grate function and feed the cabbage through the chute. Repeat the process with the bell pepper and apple. Remove the bowl and set aside.

In a separate bowl, combine the ricotta cheese, mayonnaise, vinegar, salt and caraway seeds. Add the dressing to the salad and toss to mix completely. Garnish the salad with the minced chive.

❧ SERVES 4.

Soups & Salads

Calories:. 212	Carbohydrates: . . . . 35 g.
Total Fat:. . . . . 4 g.	Protein: . . . . 14 g.
Saturated Fat:. . . . . 1 g.	Cholesterol: . . . . 11 mg.
% Calories from Fat: 16	Sodium: . . . . 585 mg.

Broccoli & Apple Cole Slaw

1/2 head	small purple cabbage
1	tart apple, halved and cored
1 cup	broccoli florets
1 clove	garlic, minced
1/4 cup	nonfat sour cream
1/4 cup	nonfat plain yogurt
1/2 cup	lowfat milk
2 tbsp.	Dijon mustard
1 tbsp.	cider vinegar
1 tsp.	salt
1/2 tsp.	pepper
2 tbsp.	roasted almonds, slivered

Attach the slicing disc to the main body of the saladXPRESS™ and fasten it to the bowl, securing the safety latches. Use the slice/grate function and feed the cabbage through the chute. Repeat the process with the apple. Remove the bowl and add the broccoli. Mix together well.

In a separate bowl, combine the garlic, sour cream, yogurt, milk, mustard, vinegar, salt and pepper. Whisk well and drizzle over the salad. Toss to coat. To serve, sprinkle the top of the salad with the slivered almonds.

SERVES 6.

Calories: 97	Carbohydrates: . . . . 17 g.
Total Fat:. . . . . 2 g.	Protein:. . . . . 5 g.
Saturated Fat:. . . . . <1 g.	Cholesterol: . . . . 4 mg.
% Calories from Fat: 20	Sodium: . . . . 499 mg.

Watercress Salad with Snow Peas & Ginger

2	carrots, peeled and steamed
2 small	red bell peppers, seeded
1/4 cup	reserved pineapple juice
2 tbsp.	white vinegar
1 tbsp.	low sodium soy sauce
1/2 tsp.	fresh gingerroot, minced
1 bunch	watercress, washed and spin-dried
20 oz.	can unsweetened pineapple rings, juice reserved
1/2 lb.	snow peas, trimmed and steamed
1 tsp.	sesame seeds

Attach the slicing disc to the main body of the saladXPRESS™ and fasten it to the bowl, securing the safety latches. Use the slice/grate function and feed the carrots and bell peppers through the chute. Remove the bowl and set aside

In a separate bowl, combine the reserved pineapple juice, vinegar, soy sauce and gingerroot. Whisk together well. To serve, line a large serving platter with the watercress. Arrange the pineapple, snow peas, carrots, and bell peppers attractively over the watercress. Cover and chill. Just before serving, pour the vinegar mixture over the salad and sprinkle with the sesame seeds.

SERVES 8.

Calories:	62	Carbohydrates:	14 g.
Total Fat:	<1 g.	Protein:	2 g.
Saturated Fat:	<1 g.	Cholesterol:	0 mg.
% Calories from Fat:	6	Sodium:	74 mg.

Oriental Bamboo Salad with Hoisin Dressing

4	romaine lettuce leaves, washed and spin-dried
1	carrot, peeled
1/2 cup	fresh or canned bamboo shoots
4 oz.	canned water chestnuts
2 ribs	celery
1 cup	mung bean sprouts
1 cup	fresh broccoli florets, washed and dried

Hoisin Dressing:

2 tbsp.	hoisin sauce
1/4 cup	sesame oil
2 tbsp.	rice vinegar
1 tbsp.	sugar
1 tsp.	salt
1/2 tsp.	black pepper

Attach the slicing disc to the main body of the saladXPRESS™ and fasten it to the bowl, securing the safety latches. Use the slice/grate function and feed the romaine lettuce through the chute. Repeat the process with the carrot, bamboo, water chestnuts, celery and sprouts. Remove the bowl and add the broccoli. Mix well and set aside.

In a separate bowl, whisk together the hoisin sauce, sesame oil, vinegar, sugar, salt and pepper. Pour the dressing over the salad and toss to coat.

❧ SERVES 6.

Calories:. 130	Carbohydrates: . . . . 11 g.
Total Fat: . . . . 10 g.	Protein: . . . . 2 g.
Saturated Fat: . . . . <1 g.	Cholesterol: . . . . <1 mg.
% Calories from Fat: 64	Sodium: . . . . 503 mg.

Cucumber & Red Onion Salad with Creamy Ginger Dressing

1	English cucumber, peeled
1 small	red onion, peeled and sectioned
2 tbsp.	freshly grated ginger
2 tsp.	lemon juice
1 1/2 tsp.	low sodium soy sauce
1 tbsp.	nonfat milk
1 clove	garlic

Attach the slicing disc to the main body of the saladXPRESS™ and fasten it to the bowl, securing the safety latches. Use the slice/grate function and feed the cucumber through the chute. Repeat the process with the red onion. Remove the bowl and set aside.

In a separate bowl, combine the ginger, lemon juice, soy sauce, milk and garlic and blend well. Pour the dressing over the salad and toss to coat. Refrigerate for 1 hour and serve.

❧ SERVES 4.

Calories: 23	Carbohydrates: . . . . 5 g.
Total Fat: . . . . <1 g.	Protein: . . . . 1 g.
Saturated Fat: . . . . <1 g.	Cholesterol: . . . . <1 mg.
% Calories from Fat: 6	Sodium: . . . . 67 mg.

Garden Flower Salad

1 cup	cherry tomatoes
2	green onions
10	walnuts, shelled
1 1/2 cups	butter lettuce, washed and spin-dried
1 cup	arugula, washed and spin-dried
1 tbsp.	oil
1 tbsp.	vinegar
1/4 cup	impatiens, or other edible flower

Attach the slicing disc to the main body of the saladXPRESS™ and fasten it to the bowl, securing the safety latches. Use the slice/grate function and feed the tomatoes and onions through the chute. Attach the grating disc and grate the walnuts. Remove the bowl and add the torn butter lettuce and arugula. Mix well. To serve, drizzle the oil and vinegar over the salad and toss to blend. Top with the fresh flowers.

SERVES 6.

Calories: 93	Carbohydrates: . . . . 4 g.
Total Fat:. . . . . 9 g.	Protein:. . . . . 2 g.
Saturated Fat:. . . . . <1 g.	Cholesterol: . . . . 0 mg.
% Calories from Fat: 77	Sodium:. . . . . 6 mg.

Spicy Milano Salad

1	red bell pepper, seeded
1	carrot, peeled
1	red onion, peeled and quartered
1 small	cucumber, peeled
8 oz.	can artichoke hearts marinated in water, drained
1/4 cup	black olives, pitted
1/4 cup	green olives, pitted
2 oz.	aged Parmesan cheese
1 small	head of romaine lettuce, washed and spin-dried, torn

Garlic Thyme Dressing:

1 sprig	fresh thyme, minced
2 cloves	garlic, minced
2 tbsp.	extra virgin olive oil
1/4 cup	balsamic vinegar
1 tbsp.	sugar
1 tsp.	dry mustard
1/2 tsp.	black pepper

Attach the slicing disc to the main body of the saladXPRESS™ and fasten it to the bowl, securing the safety latches. Use the slice/grate function and feed the red bell pepper through the chute. Repeat this process with the carrot, onion, cucumber, artichoke hearts, black and green olives. Use the grating disc to grate the cheese. Transfer the salad to a separate serving bowl; set aside.

In a separate bowl, whisk together the thyme, garlic, oil, vinegar, sugar, mustard and pepper. Pour the dressing over the salad and serve.

MAKES 6 SERVINGS.

Calories:. 162	Carbohydrates: . . . . 15 g.
Total Fat:. . . . . 9 g.	Protein:. . . . . 7 g.
Saturated Fat:. . . . . <1 g.	Cholesterol: . . . . 0 mg.
% Calories from Fat: 47	Sodium:. . . . . 342 mg.

Blue Cheese & Cranberry Salad

1/4 cup	fresh cranberries, washed
1/2 small	red onion, peeled and sectioned
1 cup	roasted almonds
1 clove	garlic
1 head	romaine lettuce, washed and spin-dried, torn
1/2 bunch	baby spinach leaves, washed and spin-dried
3 tbsp.	red vinegar
2 tbsp.	vegetable oil
1 tbsp.	Dijon mustard
1/2 tsp.	salt
1/2 tsp.	black pepper
2 tbsp.	water
4 oz.	blue cheese, crumbled
1/4 cup	dried cranberries

Attach the slicing disc to the main body of the saladXPRESS™ and fasten it to the bowl, securing the safety latches. Use the slice/grate function and feed the fresh cranberries through the chute. Repeat the process with the red onion, almonds and garlic. Remove the bowl and add the torn romaine leaves and spinach. Toss.

In a separate bowl, whisk the vinegar, oil, mustard, salt, pepper and water. Pour this dressing over the salad and toss until evenly coated. Top with the crumbled blue cheese and dried cranberries.

❧ SERVES 8.

Calories:. 212	Carbohydrates: . . . . 9 g.
Total Fat:. . . . . 17 g.	Protein:. . . . . 9 g.
Saturated Fat:. . . . . 4 g.	Cholesterol: . . . . 10 mg.
% Calories from Fat: 69	Sodium:. . . . . 433 mg.

Chile Pepper Indian Cucumber Salad

3 large	cucumbers, peeled
	salt to taste
3 tbsp.	fresh lemon juice
1 tsp.	sugar
2 tbsp.	lowfat margarine
1 tsp.	ground cumin
2	dried red chile peppers
1 tbsp.	fresh cilantro, minced
10	peanuts, chopped

Attach the slicing disc to the main body of the saladXPRESS™ and fasten it to the bowl, securing the safety latches. Use the slice/grate function and feed the cucumber through the chute. Remove the bowl and transfer the cucumber to a colander. Mix the salt with the cucumber and let it drain for 10 minutes to release the water. Place the cucumber into a serving bowl, and stir in the lemon juice and sugar. Set aside.

Melt the margarine in a small saucepan. Stir in the cumin and chili peppers and cook just until warm. Add the warm dressing to the cucumbers. Stir and toss to coat thoroughly. Garnish with the cilantro and peanuts.

SERVES 6.

Calories: 64	Carbohydrates: . . . . 7 g.
Total Fat: . . . . 4 g.	Protein: . . . . 2 g.
Saturated Fat: . . . . <1 g.	Cholesterol: . . . . 0 mg.
% Calories from Fat: 46	Sodium: . . . . 42 mg.

Mandarin Cole Slaw with Lemon Yogurt

1/2	pineapple, peeled and sectioned
1/2 head	purple cabbage, washed and cored
1 rib	celery
1	banana, peeled
11 oz.	can mandarin oranges, drained
2 tbsp.	lemon juice
1/4 cup	currants
4	walnuts, chopped
1 cup	nonfat lemon yogurt

Attach the slicing disc to the main body of the saladXPRESS™ and fasten it to the bowl, securing the safety latches. Use the slice/grate function and feed the pineapple through the chute. Repeat the process with the cabbage, celery and banana. Remove the bowl and add the oranges, lemon juice, currants and walnuts. Toss to blend. To serve, top each serving with a dollop of yogurt.

⁓❧ SERVES 6.

Calories:. 162	Carbohydrates: . . . . 36 g.
Total Fat:. . . . . 1 g.	Protein:. . . . . 4 g.
Saturated Fat:. . . . . <1 g.	Cholesterol: . . . . 0 mg.
% Calories from Fat: 7	Sodium:. . . . . 58 mg.

Tri-Apple Slaw

1/2 head	purple cabbage, washed and cored
1	Fuji apple, halved and cored
1	Granny Smith apple, halved and cored
1	Golden Delicious apple, halved and cored
1 small	carrot, peeled
1 small	red bell pepper
2	green onions
1/3 cup	lowfat sour cream
1 tbsp.	lowfat mayonnaise
1 tbsp.	brown sugar
1 tbsp.	lemon juice

Attach the slicing disc to the main body of the saladXPRESS™ and fasten it to the bowl, securing the safety latches. Use the slice/grate function and feed the cabbage through the chute. Repeat the process with the apples, carrot, bell pepper and onions. Remove the bowl and set side.

In a separate bowl, combine the sour cream, mayonnaise, brown sugar and lemon juice. Blend well. Pour the dressing over the salad and toss to coat. Chill before serving.

SERVES 6.

Calories: 130	Carbohydrates: . . . . 28 g.
Total Fat: . . . . 2 g.	Protein: . . . . 3 g.
Saturated Fat: . . . . <1 g.	Cholesterol: . . . . 4 mg.
% Calories from Fat: 12	Sodium: . . . . 61 mg.

Tomato-Bowtie Pasta Salad

2	vine-ripened tomatoes, seeded
6	pear tomatoes, seeded
1 sprig	fresh basil
1 sprig	fresh oregano
1 sprig	fresh thyme
9 oz.	pkg. bowtie pasta, cooked al dente, drained
1 tbsp.	extra virgin olive oil
2 tbsp.	red vinegar
1/4 cup	reduced-fat Romano cheese, grated

Attach the slicing disc to the main body of the saladXPRESS™ and fasten it to the bowl, securing the safety latches. Use the slice/grate function and feed the tomatoes through the chute. Attach the grating disc and feed the basil, oregano and thyme through the chute. Remove the bowl and add the pasta. Toss well. Add the oil and vinegar and toss to coat thoroughly. To serve, sprinkle with the cheese.

◆ SERVES 4.

Calories:. 260	Carbohydrates: . . . . 53 g.
Total Fat:. . . . . 6 g.	Protein: . . . . 17 g.
Saturated Fat:. . . . . 1 g.	Cholesterol: . . . . 73 mg.
% Calories from Fat: 19	Sodium: . . . . 284 mg.

Leek, Green Chile & Brown Rice Salad with Dijon Mustard

1 large	red bell pepper, seeded
1	leek, cleaned
1/4 cup	pecans, shelled
3 cups	brown rice, steamed
7 oz.	can diced green chiles, drained
1/4 cup	white vinegar
2 tbsp.	vegetable oil
1 tsp.	Dijon mustard

Attach the slicing disc to the main body of the saladXPRESS™ and fasten it to the bowl, securing the safety latches. Use the slice/grate function and feed the bell pepper through the chute. Repeat the process with the leek and pecans. Remove the bowl and add the rice. Toss to blend.

In a separate bowl, mix together the chiles, vinegar, oil and mustard. Blend well. Spoon the dressing over the salad and toss to coat.

❧ SERVES 4 TO 6.

Calories:.	207	Carbohydrates:	29 g.
Total Fat:.	9 g.	Protein:.	4 g.
Saturated Fat:.	1 g.	Cholesterol:	<1 mg.
% Calories from Fat:	38	Sodium:.	108 mg.

Fresh Harvest Salad

1 small	zucchini, peeled
1 small	yellow squash, peeled
1/2 lb.	fresh mushrooms, cleaned and stems removed
1	vine-ripened tomato, seeded
1/4	purple onion, peeled and sectioned
2 tbsp.	vegetable oil
1/4 cup	rice vinegar
1 tsp.	sugar
1 tsp.	paprika
1/2 tsp.	salt
1 tsp.	black pepper

Attach the slicing disc to the main body of the saladXPRESS™ and fasten it to the bowl, securing the safety latches. Use the slice/grate function and feed the zucchini through the chute. Repeat the process with the yellow squash, mushrooms, tomato and onion. Remove the bowl and set aside.

In a separate bowl, whisk together the oil, vinegar, sugar, paprika, salt and pepper. Pour the dressing over the salad and toss lightly. Cover and chill before serving.

❧ SERVES 4 TO 6.

Calories: 75	Carbohydrates: . . . . 6 g.
Total Fat: . . . . 5 g.	Protein: . . . . 2 g.
Saturated Fat: . . . . <1 g.	Cholesterol: . . . . 0 mg.
% Calories from Fat: 57	Sodium: . . . . 200 mg.

Chapter 5

Desserts & Bakery Goods

Fresh Mango Sorbet

3 large	mangos, peeled and cut into large pieces
2 1/2 cups	nonfat vanilla yogurt
6 tbsp.	light corn syrup
6 tbsp.	evaporated milk

Attach the grating disc to the main body of the saladXPRESS™ and fasten it to the bowl, securing the safety latches. Use the slice/grate function and feed the mangos through the chute. Add the yogurt, corn syrup and milk to the mangos and mix thoroughly. Cover and freeze in the bowl for 2 hours. Mash the sorbet with a large fork until no large lumps remain. Cover and return to the freezer for 2 hours. Mash again with a large fork. If a smoother consistency is desired, you may use a blender to process the sorbet for 1 minute at high speed. Cover and freeze for 2 hours, or until ready to serve. Mash the sorbet every 2 hours until serving.

SERVES 6 TO 8.

Calories:. 124	Carbohydrates: . . . . 22 g.
Total Fat:. . . . . 3 g.	Protein:. . . . . 4 g.
Saturated Fat:. . . . . 1 g.	Cholesterol: . . . . 38 mg.
% Calories from Fat: 27	Sodium: . . . . 371 mg.

Strawberries & Lemon Crème

8	graham cracker squares, crushed
2 tsp.	sugar
1 tbsp.	margarine, melted
2 cups	fresh whole strawberries, hulled
1/4 cup	lemon juice
1 cup	evaporated milk
8 oz.	nonfat whipped topping, thawed

Toss together the graham crackers, sugar and margarine. Spread the crumbs over the bottom of a 9-inch pie plate. Attach the slicing disc to the main body of the saladXPRESS™ and fasten it to the bowl, securing the safety latches. Use the slice/grate function and feed the strawberries through the chute.

Layer the sliced strawberries evenly over the crumbs, reserving a few for the garnish. Mix together in a medium bowl the lemon juice and milk. Add the whipped topping and spoon over the strawberries. Cover and freeze for at least 6 hours or up to 12 hours. Add the remaining strawberries to garnish before serving.

❧ SERVES 8.

Calories: 64	Carbohydrates: . . . . 39 g.
Total Fat:. . . . . 3 g.	Protein:. . . . . 2 g.
Saturated Fat:. . . . . <1 g.	Cholesterol: . . . . 8 mg.
% Calories from Fat: 24	Sodium:. . . . . 189 mg.

Banana Crème Parfaits

3 small	bananas, peeled
1 loaf	prepared lowfat pound cake, cut into 1/2-inch thick slices
4 oz.	pkg. instant nonfat banana pudding, prepared as directed
1/4 cup	fat free chocolate syrup

Attach the slicing disc to the main body of the saladXPRESS™ and fasten it to the bowl, securing the safety latches. Use the slice/grate function and feed the bananas through the chute. Using 6 glass parfait glasses, line the edges of the glasses with pound cake slices. Layer the bananas and banana pudding in the middle of the cake slices. Drizzle the chocolate syrup over each parfait to serve.

❧ MAKES 6 PARFAITS.

Calories:. 202	Carbohydrates: . . . . 43 g.
Total Fat:. . . . . 7 g.	Protein:. . . . . 2 g.
Saturated Fat:. . . . . 2 g.	Cholesterol: . . . . 22 mg.
% Calories from Fat: 37	Sodium:. . . . . 269 mg.

Cinnamon & Spice
Green Apple Streusel

2 1/2 lbs.	tart green apples, peeled, halved and cored
3/4 cup	all-purpose flour
1/2 cup	dry buttermilk
1/2 cup	dark brown sugar, firmly packed
2 tsp.	ground cinnamon
1/4 tsp.	ground ginger
1/2 cup	lowfat margarine

Attach the slicing disc to the main body of the saladXPRESS™ and fasten it to the bowl, securing the safety latches. Use the slice/grate function and feed the apples through the chute. Thinly slice the apples, and place them in a 2 1/2-quart baking dish.

Preheat the oven to 300°F. In a separate bowl, combine the flour, dry buttermilk, brown sugar, cinnamon and ginger. Stir to combine well. Using a pastry cutter, cut the margarine into the flour mixture until it resembles coarse crumbs. Stir 1/3-cup of the dough into the sliced apples. Press the remaining dough into small portions. Break the portions into 3/4-inch chunks over the apples. Bake, uncovered, 40 to 50 minutes until the apples are tender and the streusel is golden.

⤷ SERVES 6 TO 8.

Calories:. 254		Carbohydrates: . . . . 6 g.	
Total Fat:. . . . . 20 g.		Protein: . . . . 15 g.	
Saturated Fat:. . . . . 1 g.		Cholesterol: . . . . 18 mg.	
% Calories from Fat: 68		Sodium:. . . . . 622 mg.	

Orange Cranberry Cookies

2 1/4 cups	fresh cranberries, rinsed
2 cups	walnuts
1/2 cup	lowfat margarine, softened
1 cup	sugar
3/4 cup	dark brown sugar, firmly packed
1/4 cup	nonfat milk
1	egg (use egg substitute, if desired)
2 tbsp.	orange juice
1 tbsp.	orange rind, grated
3 cups	all-purpose flour
1/2 tsp.	baking powder
1/4 tsp.	baking soda
1/2 tsp.	salt

Place the cranberries in the basket of the saladXPRESS™ and rinse them in fresh water. Use the Spin Dry function to spin the cranberries for 10 seconds to remove any excess moisture. Remove the cranberries. Attach the grating disc to the saladXPRESS™. Grate the cranberries and set aside. Grate the walnuts and set aside.

Preheat the oven to 375°F. In a mixing bowl, cream the margarine and sugars until fluffy. Add the milk, egg, orange juice and rind. Beat well. In a separate bowl, combine the flour, baking powder, baking soda and salt. Add the dry ingredients to the creamed margarine and stir thoroughly. Stir in the cranberries and walnuts by hand.

Drop the dough by rounded teaspoonfuls onto cookie sheets that have been coated with nonstick cooking spray and bake for 12 to 14 minutes. The cookies will be lightly browned when done. Cool slightly on the cookie sheets. Place the cookies on wire racks to finish cooling. Store in an airtight container.

❧ 2 COOKIES PER SERVING.

Calories:. 100	Carbohydrates: . . . . 16 g.
Total Fat:. . . . . 4 g.	Protein:. . . . . 2 g.
Saturated Fat:. . . . . <1 g.	Cholesterol: . . . . 5 mg.
% Calories from Fat: 33	Sodium:. . . . . 60 mg.

Fresh Plum Cobbler

12 large	firm, ripe plums, pitted
1/4 tsp.	ground allspice
1/4 tsp.	ground nutmeg
1/4 cup	quick-cooking tapioca
1/4 cup	apple juice
2 3 oz.	pkgs. nonfat cream cheese, softened
1/2 cup	lowfat margarine
2 tbsp.	sugar
1 1/2 cups	all-purpose flour
2 tbsp.	lowfat milk

Attach the slicing disc to the main body of the saladXPRESS™ and fasten it to the bowl, securing the safety latches. Use the slice/grate function and feed the plums through the chute. Thinly slice the plums. Add the allspice, nutmeg, quick-cooking tapioca and the apple juice to the plum slices and stir to combine. Let sit for 1 hour.

In a small bowl, beat the cream cheese, margarine and sugar with an electric mixer until smooth and creamy. Add the flour and mix completely. Pat the dough out to a 1-inch thickness, wrap in plastic wrap and chill for 30 minutes. Preheat the oven to 350°F. On a lightly floured surface, roll the dough out to fit a 9" x 13" baking pan. Pour the plum mixture into the baking pan and place the dough on top of the fruit. Lightly brush the milk over the top of the dough, and cut several slashes in the dough to allow steam to escape. Bake for 60 to 80 minutes, until the top is golden brown.

❧ SERVES 9 TO 10.

Calories:	131	Carbohydrates:	32 g.
Total Fat:	3 g.	Protein:	6 g.
Saturated Fat:	1 g.	Cholesterol:	4 mg.
% Calories from Fat:	16	Sodium:	198 mg.

Pineapple & Walnut Carrot Cake

10 large	carrots, peeled
2 cups	all-purpose flour
1/2 cup	sugar
2 tsp.	baking soda
1 tsp.	ground cinnamon
1 tsp.	salt
1 cup	unsweetened applesauce
4	eggs (use egg substitute, if desired)
6 1/4 oz.	can crushed pineapple
1/2 cup	walnuts
	powdered sugar for dusting

Preheat the oven to 350°F. Coat a 9" x 13" baking pan with nonstick cooking spray and sprinkle with flour. Attach the grating disc to the main body of the saladXPRESS™ and fasten it to the bowl, securing the safety latches. Use the slice/grate function and feed the carrots through the chute. In a separate bowl, combine the flour, sugar, baking soda, cinnamon and salt. Add the applesauce, eggs, carrots and pineapple and beat well after each addition. Attach the grating disc to the saladXPRESS™ and grate the walnuts. Add the walnuts to the batter. Pour the batter into the prepared baking pan. Bake for 35 minutes. Remove from the oven and cool on a wire rack. Dust the top of the cake with powdered sugar.

Desserts & Bakery Goods

 SERVES 12.

Calories:. 254	Carbohydrates: . . . . 6 g.
Total Fat:. . . . . 20 g.	Protein: . . . . 15 g.
Saturated Fat:. . . . . 1 g.	Cholesterol: . . . . 18 mg.
% Calories from Fat: 68	Sodium: . . . . 622 mg.

Quick Caramel Baked Pears

4	bartlett pears, cored and cut in half
1/4 cup	prepared caramel topping
pinch	ground cinnamon
1/4 cup	fresh pineapple juice

Attach the slicing disc to the main body of the saladXPRESS™ and fasten it to the bowl, securing the safety latches. Use the slice/grate function and feed the pears through the chute. Place the pear slices in a 2-quart baking dish and drizzle the caramel topping over the slices. Sprinkle with the cinnamon. Pour the pineapple juice into the bottom of the pan and cover tightly with foil. Bake at 350°F for 15 to 20 minutes, until the pears are softened and warm.

❧ SERVES 6.

Calories:. 337	Carbohydrates: . . . . 50 g.
Total Fat: . . . . 12 g.	Protein: . . . . 7 g.
Saturated Fat:. . . . . 5 g.	Cholesterol: . . . . 69 mg.
% Calories from Fat: 32	Sodium: . . . . 200 mg.

Fresh Rhubarb & Strawberry Trifle

12 ribs	fresh rhubarb, cut into 2-inch lengths
1 cup	fresh strawberries, washed and hulled
1/3 cup	water
1 tbsp.	cornstarch
2 tbsp.	water
1/4 cup	sugar
8 oz.	nonfat whipped topping
1 loaf	nonfat pound cake

Attach the slicing disc to the main body of the saladXPRESS™ and fasten it to the bowl, securing the safety latches. Use the slice/grate function and feed the rhubarb through the chute. Repeat the process with the strawberries.

Place the fruit in a medium saucepan and heat with the water until the water boils. Stir together the cornstarch and 2 tablespoons of water until smooth and add to the fruit. Cook and stir over medium heat until thickened. Add the sugar and cook until the sugar dissolves. Remove the fruit from the heat and cool.

To assemble, layer the fruit and sauce with the cake and whipped topping in a large serving bowl. Cover and chill.

SERVES 12.

Calories:. 254	Carbohydrates: . . . . 6 g.
Total Fat: . . . . 20 g.	Protein: . . . . 15 g.
Saturated Fat:. . . . . 1 g.	Cholesterol: . . . . 18 mg.
% Calories from Fat: 68	Sodium: . . . . 622 mg.

Fresh Fruit Tart with Pineapple Glaze

Crust:

3/4 cup	lowfat margarine
1/3 cup	powdered sugar
1 1/2 cups	all-purpose flour

Filling:

8 oz.	nonfat cream cheese, softened
1/2 cup	sugar
1 tsp.	vanilla extract
2	fresh kiwis, peeled
2	pears, peeled
2	bananas, peeled
12	strawberries, washed and hulled
1 cup	raspberries

Glaze:

2 tbsp.	cornstarch
1 cup	pineapple juice
1/2 cup	sugar
1 tsp.	lemon juice

Preheat the oven to 300°F. Coat a 12-inch pizza pan with nonstick cooking spray. In a small bowl, combine the margarine, powdered sugar and flour until crumbly. Press into the pizza pan and bake for 25 to 30 minutes. Cool before adding the topping.

In a small bowl, combine the cream cheese, sugar and the vanilla. Spread the cream cheese mixture on the cooled crust. Attach the slicing disc to the main body of the saladXPRESS™ and fasten it to the bowl, securing the safety latches. Use the slice/grate function and feed the kiwis through the chute. Repeat the process with the pears, bananas, and strawberries. Arrange all of the fruit artistically on the cream cheese spread.

In a small saucepan over medium heat, combine the cornstarch, pineapple juice, sugar and lemon juice until it thickens. Remove from the heat and let it stand for a few minutes. Spoon the glaze over the fruit tart.

~& SERVES 12.

Calories:. 256	Carbohydrates: . . . . 53 g.
Total Fat:. . . . . 4 g.	Protein:. . . . . 5 g.
Saturated Fat:. . . . . 1 g.	Cholesterol: . . . . 3 mg.
% Calories from Fat: 12	Sodium:. . . . . 228 mg.

Desserts & Bakery Goods

Vanilla Flan with Strawberry Compote

Strawberry Compote:

2 pints	strawberries, rinsed and hulled
1/4 cup	sugar
1/2 cup	strawberry-flavored syrup

Flan:

1/3 cup	sugar
2 tbsp.	cornstarch
1/4 tsp.	salt
2 cups	light cream
1 tsp.	vanilla extract
1 tbsp.	dark brown sugar, packed

Attach the slicing disc to the main body of the saladXPRESS™ and fasten it to the bowl, securing the safety latches. Use the slice/grate function and feed the strawberries through the chute. In a non-reactive saucepan, over low heat, combine the strawberries, sugar and the syrup. Stir and simmer until the compote is slightly thickened. Cool, cover and chill until ready to serve.

To prepare the flan, combine the sugar, cornstarch and salt in a medium saucepan. Add the cream and heat almost to a boil over medium heat. Add the vanilla. Stir until the flan is thickened. Spoon the flan into a glass serving pan or bowl. Cover tightly and refrigerate for at least 1 hour. To serve, spoon the flan into individual bowls and top with the strawberry compote.

✤ SERVES 10 TO 12.

Calories: 193	*Carbohydrates:* . . . . 27 g.
Total Fat: . . . . 8 g.	*Protein:* . . . . 2 g.
Saturated Fat: . . . . 5 g.	*Cholesterol:* . . . . 26 mg.
% Calories from Fat: 36	*Sodium:* . . . . 66 mg.

Desserts & Bakery Goods

Tangy Lemon Galette with Strawberries

Almond Crust:

1/4 cup	almonds, shelled
1 cup	all-purpose flour
1/4 cup	sugar
1/4 tsp.	salt
6 tbsp.	lowfat margarine
1/2 tsp.	almond extract
4 tbsp.	cold water

Lemon Filling:

3	eggs (use egg substitute, if desired)
1 cup	sugar
1/2 cup	lemon juice
1 tbsp.	lemon zest
1/8 tsp.	salt
6 tbsp.	lowfat margarine
2 pints	fresh strawberries, washed and hulled

Attach the grating disc to the main body of the saladXPRESS™ and fasten it to the bowl, securing the safety latches. Use the slice/grate function and feed the almonds through the chute. Remove the bowl and add the flour, sugar and salt. Mix together with a fork and add the margarine, almond extract and water. Toss again with a fork. Lightly press the crust into a 9-inch tart pan or pie plate that has been coated with nonstick cooking spray. Bake at 425°F for 15 to 20 minutes. Cool.

Whisk together the eggs, sugar, lemon juice and zest in a saucepan over medium heat. Add the salt and margarine and stir until the filling thickens slightly. Pour the filling into the prepared galette crust. Bake at 325°F for 10 to 15 minutes, until the filling is set.

Attach the slicing disc to the saladXPRESS™ and slice the strawberries. Arrange the strawberries over the cooled tart.

🍂 SERVES 12.

Calories:. 213	Carbohydrates: . . . . 35 g.
Total Fat:. . . . . 7 g.	Protein:. . . . . 4 g.
Saturated Fat:. . . . . 2 g.	Cholesterol: . . . . 53 mg.
% Calories from Fat: 26	Sodium: . . . . 200 mg.

Spiced Peach Pie

5 medium	peaches, halved, pitted and peeled
3/4 cup	dark brown sugar, packed
3 tbsp.	all-purpose flour
1/2 tsp.	ground cinnamon
1/8 tsp.	ground cloves
pinch	salt
2 tbsp.	vanilla extract
1 tsp.	fresh lemon juice
1 tbsp.	lowfat margarine
1	9-inch reduced-fat pie shell

Preheat the oven to 375°F. Attach the slicing disc to the main body of the saladXPRESS™ and fasten it to the bowl, securing the safety latches. Use the slice/grate function and feed the peaches through the chute.

Mix together the brown sugar, flour, cinnamon, cloves and salt. Reserve 2 tablespoons and add the remaining sugar mixture to the sliced peaches. Add the vanilla and lemon juice to the peaches and toss lightly to combine. Place the peach filling in the pie crust. Dot the margarine over the top of the filling. Crumble the remaining flour and spices over the peaches. Bake for 10 minutes and reduce the heat to 350°F. Continue baking for 50 minutes, or until the peaches are tender.

⮆ SERVES 8 TO 10.

Calories:.	187	Carbohydrates:	36 g.
Total Fat:.	4 g.	Protein:.	2 g.
Saturated Fat:.	<1 g.	Cholesterol:	0 mg.
% Calories from Fat:	19	Sodium:	102 mg.

Papaya & Pineapple Parfaits

1/2	fresh pineapple, peeled and cored
1	papaya, peeled and seeded
3	kiwi fruits, peeled
4	figs, peeled
1/2	honeydew melon, peeled and seeded
1/2 tsp.	almond extract
8 oz.	nonfat vanilla yogurt
1/4 cup	lowfat granola

Attach the slicing disc to the main body of the saladXPRESS™ and fasten it to the bowl, securing the safety latches. Use the slice/grate function and feed the pineapple through the chute. Repeat the process with the papaya, kiwi, figs and melon.

Mix together the almond extract and yogurt. To assemble, layer the mixed fruit with the yogurt and granola in parfait glasses.

❧ SERVES 8.

Calories:. 145		Carbohydrates: . . . . 34 g.
Total Fat: . . . . <1 g.		Protein: . . . . 3 g.
Saturated Fat: . . . . <1 g.		Cholesterol: . . . . <1 mg.
% Calories from Fat: 4		Sodium: . . . . 39 mg.

Cinnamon-Spiced Pineapple Upside Down Cake

1	ripe pineapple, peeled and cored
1/4 cup	lowfat margarine
2/3 cup	light brown sugar, packed
1/3 cup	pecan halves
1 cup	all-purpose flour
3/4 cup	sugar
1 1/2 tsp.	baking powder
1/2 tsp.	salt
1/2 tsp.	ground cinnamon
1/4 tsp.	allspice
1/4 cup	shortening
1/2 cup	lowfat milk
1	egg
2 tbsp.	pineapple juice

Attach the slicing disc to the main body of the saladXPRESS™ and fasten it to the bowl, securing the safety latches. Use the slice/grate function and feed the pineapple through the chute. Slice the pineapple into 1/2-inch thick slices.

Preheat the oven to 350°F. In a heavy ovenproof 10-inch skillet, melt the margarine over medium heat. Add the brown sugar and stir until dissolved. Remove from the heat. Arrange the pineapple slices in concentric circles on top of the sugar mixture, using as many pineapple slices as possible. Place the pecan halves around the pineapple. Set aside.

In a medium bowl, combine the flour, sugar, baking powder, salt, cinnamon and allspice. Add the shortening and milk and beat until smooth. Add the egg and the pineapple juice and beat for 2 minutes. Gently pour the batter over the pineapple slices, and spread evenly. Bake 40 to 45 minutes until golden brown. Place the skillet on a wire rack to cool for 5 minutes. Invert the cake onto a serving platter.

~❧ SERVES 10 TO 12.

Calories:. 230	Carbohydrates: . . . . 39 g.
Total Fat:. . . . . 8 g.	Protein:. . . . . 2 g.
Saturated Fat:. . . . . 2 g.	Cholesterol: . . . . 19 mg.
% Calories from Fat: 31	Sodium:. . . . . 200 mg.

Pineapple Banana Meringue

Meringue:

3	egg whites, beaten until stiff
2 tbsp.	sugar
1/4 tsp.	vanilla extract
dash	salt
1/8 tsp.	cream of tartar

Banana Filling:

3 large	bananas, peeled
2 cups	fresh pineapple, cut in large chunks
2 oz.	pkg. sugar-free instant vanilla pudding
3 cups	nonfat milk

1 sprig	fresh mint leaves for garnish

Preheat the oven to 300°F. Use an electric mixer to beat the egg whites and sugar until very stiff. Add the vanilla, salt and cream of tartar. Spoon the meringue into a 9-inch pie plate that has been coated with nonstick cooking spray. Spread the meringue over the bottom and sides of the plate evenly. Bake for 45 minutes. Cool.

Attach the slicing disc to the main body of the saladXPRESS™ and fasten it to the bowl, securing the safety latches. Use the slice/grate function and feed the bananas through the chute. Repeat with the pineapple. Prepare the pudding using the nonfat milk. Fold the bananas and pineapple into the prepared pudding, mixing well. Pour the fruit and pudding into the meringue shell. Chill for 1 hour before serving. Garnish with mint leaves.

🖋 SERVES 8.

Calories: *126*	*Carbohydrates:* . . . . *26 g.*
Total Fat: . . . . *<1 g.*	*Protein:* . . . . *<1 g.*
Saturated Fat: . . . . *0 g.*	*Cholesterol:* . . . . *0 mg.*
% Calories from Fat: *16*	*Sodium:* . . . . *115 mg.*

Glazed Apple Pizza

1 1/4 cups	all-purpose flour
1/2 tsp.	salt
1/2 cup	shortening
1/4 cup	milk
1	egg yolk
6	tart apples, peeled, cored and halved
1 cup	cornflakes, crushed
3/4 cup	sugar
2 tsp.	ground cinnamon

Glaze:

1/2 cup	powdered sugar
1 tsp.	vanilla extract
2 tsp.	hot water

Combine the flour and salt in a medium bowl. Cut in the shortening until the mixture is coarse crumbs. Whisk together the milk and egg yolk and add to the flour until a soft dough forms. Cover and chill for 1 hour.

Preheat the oven to 350°F. Attach the slicing disc to the main body of the saladXPRESS™ and fasten it to the bowl, securing the safety latches. Use the slice/grate function and feed the apples through the chute. Set aside.

On a lightly floured board, roll half of the dough out to fit a 13-inch pizza pan. Sprinkle the dough with cornflakes. Top with the sliced apples. Combine the sugar and cinnamon and sprinkle over the apples. Bake for 40 to 45 minutes, until golden brown.

Combine the powdered sugar and vanilla. Stir in just enough hot water to make a glaze. Drizzle over the warm pizza.

SERVES 10.

Calories:. 270	Carbohydrates: . . . . 46 g.
Total Fat:. . . . . 9 g.	Protein:. . . . . 2 g.
Saturated Fat:. . . . . 2 g.	Cholesterol: . . . . 18 mg.
% Calories from Fat: 30	Sodium:. . . . . 126 mg.

Parmesan Cheese Bread

1/2 cup	nonfat milk
1/4 oz.	active dry yeast
2 1/4 cups	all-purpose flour, divided
6 tbsp.	chilled lowfat margarine
4 oz.	Parmesan cheese
2 tbsp.	sugar
1/2 tsp.	salt
2 large	eggs (use egg substitute, if desired)

In a small saucepan over low heat, heat the milk until it is warm. Remove from the heat. Whisk in the yeast and 1 cup flour. Cover and let it sit until foamy. Attach the grating disc to the main body of the saladXPRESS™ and fasten it to the bowl, securing the safety latches. Use the slice/grate function and feed the margarine through the chute. Repeat the process with the Parmesan cheese. Remove the bowl. Add the sugar and salt to the butter and cheese, mixing until it is soft and smooth. Add the eggs, one at a time, mixing after each addition. Add the remaining flour and the yeast mixture and stir to form a soft, smooth dough.

Turn the dough out onto a floured surface and knead several times. Press it into a rough square and round the corners to fit a 9-inch cake pan. Place the dough in a 9-inch cake pan that has been coated with nonstick cooking spray, cover and let it rise until it has doubled in size, about an hour. Preheat the oven to 350°F. Bake the bread for 40 minutes, or until it is a deep golden color. Turn the bread onto a wire rack to cool.

Calories:. 160	Carbohydrates: . . . . 21 g.
Total Fat:. . . . . 5 g.	Protein:. . . . . 7 g.
Saturated Fat:. . . . . <1 g.	Cholesterol: . . . . 42 mg.
% Calories from Fat: 28	Sodium: . . . . 318 mg.

Desserts &
Bakery Goods

Sharp Cheddar & Caraway Crackers

8 oz.	sharp cheddar cheese
1 cup	lowfat margarine, softened
1 tbsp.	fresh chives, chopped
1 tsp.	caraway seeds
1/2 tsp.	dry mustard
1/8 tsp.	ground red pepper
1 tsp.	Worcestershire sauce
2 2/3 cups	all-purpose flour

Attach the grating disc to the main body of the saladXPRESS™ and fasten it to the bowl, securing the safety latches. Use the slice/grate function and feed the cheese through the chute. Set the grated cheese aside.

In a large mixing bowl, whip the margarine and gradually add the cheese, chives, caraway seeds, dry mustard, red pepper and the Worcestershire sauce, beating well with an electric mixer. Gradually stir in the flour. Shape the dough into four 7-inch rolls and wrap each in waxed paper. Chill for at least 3 hours.

Preheat the oven to 375°F. Unwrap the rolls and cut the dough into 1/4-inch slices. Place the slices on greased baking sheets. Bake for 18 to 20 minutes, until the crackers are lightly browned. Let the crackers cool completely on the baking sheets and store in an airtight container.

SERVES 15.

Calories:.	169	Carbohydrates:	18 g.
Total Fat:.	8 g.	Protein:	6 g.
Saturated Fat:.	1 g.	Cholesterol:	16 mg.
% Calories from Fat:	44	Sodium:	218 mg.

Chapter 6

Super Fast
& Fresh

B.L.T. & Blue Cheese Salad

4 slices	lean turkey bacon, crisply cooked
2	green onions
1 large	tomato, seeded
2	eggs, hard boiled and peeled
10 cups	mixed salad greens
1/4 cup	blue cheese, crumbled
1/2 cup	prepared lowfat blue cheese dressing

Attach the slicing disc to the main body of the saladXPRESS™ and fasten it to the bowl, securing the safety latches. Use the slice/grate function and feed the bacon through the chute. Repeat the process with the onions, tomato and eggs. To serve, divide the lettuce greens evenly among four individual plates. Layer the eggs, green onions, tomatoes, bacon and blue cheese over each. Drizzle the blue cheese salad dressing over all.

SERVES 4.

Calories:. 167	Carbohydrates: . . . . 12 g.
Total Fat:. . . . . 10 g.	Protein: . . . . 11 g.
Saturated Fat:. . . . . 5 g.	Cholesterol:. . . . . 132 mg.
% Calories from Fat: 49	Sodium: . . . . 954 mg.

Ripe Tomato & Pepper Salad

3 small	*ripe tomatoes, seeded*
1 medium	*green bell pepper, seeded*
1 medium	*red bell pepper, seeded*
1 small	*yellow squash*
1/2 small	*purple onion, peeled and cut in half*

Herb Dressing:

1/4 cup	*prepared red vinaigrette*
1 tbsp.	*fresh parsley, minced*
1 tbsp.	*fresh basil, minced*

Attach the slicing disc to the main body of the saladXPRESS™ and fasten it to the bowl, securing the safety latches. Use the slice/grate function and feed the tomatoes through the chute. Repeat the process with the bell peppers, squash and onion. Toss the vegetables together lightly.

In a separate bowl, whisk together the vinaigrette, parsley and basil. Pour the dressing over the salad and toss.

SERVES 6 TO 8.

Calories: *57*	*Carbohydrates:* . . . . *3 g.*
Total Fat: . . . . *5 g.*	*Protein:* . . . . *<1 g.*
Saturated Fat: . . . . *1 g.*	*Cholesterol:* . . . . *0 mg.*
% Calories from Fat: *74*	*Sodium:* . . . . *111 mg.*

Super Fast
& Fresh

Spicy Blue Cheese Bruschetta

7-oz.	jar roasted red peppers, drained
2	green onions
2 cloves	garlic, minced
2 tbsp.	extra virgin olive oil, divided
1 tsp.	lemon juice
4 oz.	blue cheese
1	loaf French bread, cut into 1/2-inch slices

Attach the slicing disc to the main body of the saladXPRESS™ and fasten it to the bowl, securing the safety latches. Use the slice/grate function and feed the red peppers through the food chute. Repeat the process with the green onions. Remove the bowl and add the garlic, 1 tablespoon of olive oil, lemon juice and cheese. Mix together thoroughly. Lightly brush the slices of bread with the rest of the olive oil and place on a baking sheet. Broil until lightly toasted. Place the roasted pepper mixture on each slice and top each with 1 tablespoon of the blue cheese. Serve immediately.

⌐● MAKES 15 SLICES.

Calories:. 126	Carbohydrates: . . . . 16 g.
Total Fat:. . . . . 5 g.	Protein:. . . . . 4 g.
Saturated Fat:. . . . . <1 g.	Cholesterol: . . . . 6 mg.
% Calories from Fat: 35	Sodium:. . . . . 435 mg.

Triple J Ranch
Barbecue Chicken Salad

2	boneless, skinless chicken breast halves, cooked
4 ribs	celery
1 large	red bell pepper, seeded
1/2	red onion, peeled and cut in half
1/4 cup	prepared barbecue sauce
1 tbsp.	lowfat mayonnaise
1 tbsp.	lowfat sour cream

Attach the slicing disc to the main body of the saladXPRESS™ and fasten it to the bowl, securing the safety latches. Use the slice/grate function and feed the chicken through the chute. Repeat the process with the celery, bell pepper and onion. Remove the bowl and toss to blend.

In a separate bowl, combine the barbecue sauce, mayonnaise and sour cream. Mix well and pour over the chicken and vegetables. Toss again and refrigerate for 1 hour. Serve over a bed of greens, if desired.

SERVES 4 TO 6.

Calories: 63	Carbohydrates: . . . . 7 g.
Total Fat: . . . . 1 g.	Protein: . . . . 7 g.
Saturated Fat: . . . . <1 g.	Cholesterol: . . . . 15 mg.
% Calories from Fat: 16	Sodium: . . . . 166 mg.

Super Fast
& Fresh

Red Grape & Melon Chicken Salad

2	boneless skinless chicken breasts, cooked
1	honeydew melon, peeled and pulp removed
2 ribs	celery
1 cup	red grapes, seedless
1/2 cup	cashews
1 cup	orzo pasta, cooked al dente and rinsed

Citrus Dressing:

2 tbsp.	oil
3 tbsp.	orange juice
1/2 tsp.	salt
1/2 cup	nonfat mayonnaise
1/2 cup	nonfat plain yogurt
2 tbsp.	nonfat milk

Attach the slicing disc to the main body of the saladXPRESS™ and fasten it to the bowl, securing the safety latches. Use the slice/grate function and feed the chicken through the chute. Repeat the process with the melon, celery, grapes and cashews. Remove the bowl, add the pasta and set aside.

In a separate bowl, whisk together the oil, orange juice, salt, mayonnaise, yogurt and milk. Fold the dressing into the salad and toss well. Chill before serving.

Calories: *296*	*Carbohydrates:* . . . . *41 g.*
Total Fat: . . . . *11 g.*	*Protein:* . . . . *12 g.*
Saturated Fat: . . . . *2 g.*	*Cholesterol:* . . . . *15 mg.*
% Calories from Fat: *31*	*Sodium:* . . . . *428 mg.*

Chicken & Cheese Nachos

2	boneless, skinless chicken breast halves, grilled
3	green onions
3/4 cup	lowfat cheddar cheese
3.5 oz.	can sliced black olives
	Chile Verde Salsa (p. 30) for garnish
8 oz.	baked lowfat tortilla chips

Attach the slicing disc to the main body of the saladXPRESS™ and fasten it to the bowl, securing the safety latches. Use the slice/grate function and feed the chicken through the chute, slicing in thin strips. Remove the chicken. Slice the green onions. Use the grating disc and shred the cheese.

To serve, arrange the tortilla chips on a platter. Top the chips with the sliced chicken, cheese, green onions, olives and the Chile Verde Salsa to taste.

SERVES 4.

Calories:. 157	Carbohydrates: . . . . 29 g.
Total Fat:. . . . . 8 g.	Protein: . . . . 13 g.
Saturated Fat:. . . . . 3 g.	Cholesterol: . . . . 29 mg.
% Calories from Fat: 27	Sodium: . . . . 530 mg.

Chilled Fresh Vegetable Gazpacho

2 ribs	celery
2	cucumbers, peeled and quartered
2	green onions
1 sprig	fresh parsley
3 cups	spicy tomato juice
1/2 tsp.	Worcestershire sauce

Attach the slicing disc to the main body of the saladXPRESS™ and fasten it to the bowl, securing the safety latches. Use the slice/grate function and feed the celery through the chute. Repeat the process with the cucumbers, green onions and fresh parsley. In a large glass bowl, combine the vegetables, tomato juice and the Worcestershire sauce. Stir and refrigerate for at least 4 hours. Serve cold.

❧ SERVES 4.

Calories: 88	Carbohydrates: . . . . 36 g.
Total Fat:. . . . . 1 g.	Protein:. . . . . 2 g.
Saturated Fat:. . . . . 0 g.	Cholesterol: . . . . 17 mg.
% Calories from Fat: 27	Sodium: . . . . 544 mg.

Baked Basil Salmon & Asparagus

1 lb.	fresh asparagus, woody stems removed
2	russet potatoes, peeled and quartered
1 sprig	fresh basil
4	6 oz. salmon fillets
	salt and pepper to taste
1 tbsp.	extra virgin olive oil
	nonfat cooking spray

Attach the slicing disc to the main body of the saladXPRESS™ and fasten it to the bowl, securing the safety latches. Use the slice/grate function and feed the asparagus through the chute. Repeat the process with the potatoes and basil. Preheat the oven to 350°F. Cut 4 18-inch squares of foil. Spray the foil with the cooking spray. Place on each foil a piece of fish. Evenly divide the asparagus, potatoes and basil and place on the fish. Salt and pepper each to taste and drizzle each serving with the oil. Fold the edges of the foil together, leaving a small place for steam to escape. Place the foil packages on a baking sheet and cook for 35 to 40 minutes, until the fish flakes easily.

❧ SERVES 4.

Calories:. 279		Carbohydrates: . . . . 28 g.	
Total Fat:. . . . . 7 g.		Protein: . . . . 18 g.	
Saturated Fat:. . . . . 5 g.		Cholesterol: . . . . 27 mg.	
% Calories from Fat: 55		Sodium:. . . . . 277 mg.	

Summer Pasta Primavera

2 cups	sliced vegetables of choice: squash, carrots, green beans, mushrooms, onions
1/4 cup	Parmesan cheese
8 oz.	spaghetti, uncooked
2 tbsp.	extra virgin olive oil
1/8 tsp.	freshly ground black pepper

Attach the slicing disc to the main body of the saladXPRESS™ and fasten it to the bowl, securing the safety latches. Use the slice/grate function and feed the vegetables through the chute. Remove the vegetables to a colander. Use the grating disc and grate the Parmesan cheese. Set aside. Cook the pasta according to the directions and drain it over the vegetables in the colander. Transfer the vegetables and pasta to a serving bowl.

Drizzle with the olive oil, tossing to coat. Sprinkle with the cheese and black pepper.

SERVES 4.

Calories:. 349	Carbohydrates: . . . . 27 g.
Total Fat:. . . . . 12 g.	Protein:. . . . . 8 g.
Saturated Fat:. . . . . 6 g.	Cholesterol: . . . . 6 mg.
% Calories from Fat: 31	Sodium:. . . . . 465 mg.

Strawberry & Banana Float

2 cups	fresh ripe strawberries and bananas
1 liter	low-calorie ginger ale
2 cups	rainbow sherbert
	mint sprigs for garnish

Attach the slicing disc to the main body of the saladXPRESS™ and fasten it to the bowl, securing the safety latches. Use the slice/grate function and feed the fruit through the chute. Divide the sliced fruit among 4 tall glasses. Cover the fruit with ginger ale, filling the glass almost completely. Top each glass with a scoop of sherbet and a sprig of mint to garnish.

MAKES 4 SERVINGS.

Calories: 172	Carbohydrates: . . . . 39 g.
Total Fat: . . . . 2 g.	Protein: . . . . 2 g.
Saturated Fat: . . . . 1 g.	Cholesterol: . . . . 5 mg.
% Calories from Fat: . . . . <1	Sodium: . . . . 83 mg.

Index

RECIPE NAME:

Ingredients:

Directions:

RECIPE NAME:

Ingredients:

Directions:

RECIPE NAME:

Ingredients:

Directions:

RECIPE NAME:

Ingredients:

Directions:

RECIPE NAME:

Ingredients:

Directions:

RECIPE NAME:

Ingredients:

Directions:

RECIPE NAME:

Ingredients:

Directions:

RECIPE NAME:

Ingredients:

Directions:

RECIPE NAME:

Ingredients:

Directions:

RECIPE NAME:

Ingredients:

Directions: